AF424525

Reprints from the Royal Engineers Journal
By pagesofpages.com

Green, Miriam. *A Lady's Experiences in the Great Siege of Gibraltar (1779-83). The Journal of Miriam Green, wife of Lieut.-Colonel Green, Chief Engineer of Gibraltar.* Edited by Col. E. R. Kenyon, R. E. ii, 114 p. ISBN 979-8-9899308-0-7.

Reprinted from the Royal Engineers Journal Vols. XV and XVI, 1912.

Jones, Rice. *An Engineer Officer Under Wellington in the Peninsular. The Diary and Correspondence of Lieut. Rice Jones, R.E., During 1808-9-10-11-12.* Edited by Commander the Hon. Henry N. Shore, Late R.N. iii, 122p. ISBN 979-8-9855566-7-4. Also available as a Kindle e-book.

Reprinted from the Royal Engineers Journal Vols. XVI and XVII, 1912-13.

Thackeray, Edward T. *Sieges and the Defence of Fortified Places by the British and Indian Armies in the XIXth Century.* iii, 329p. ISBN 979-8-9855566-8-1.

Reprinted from the Royal Engineers Journal Vols. XIX to XXIII, 1914-1916.

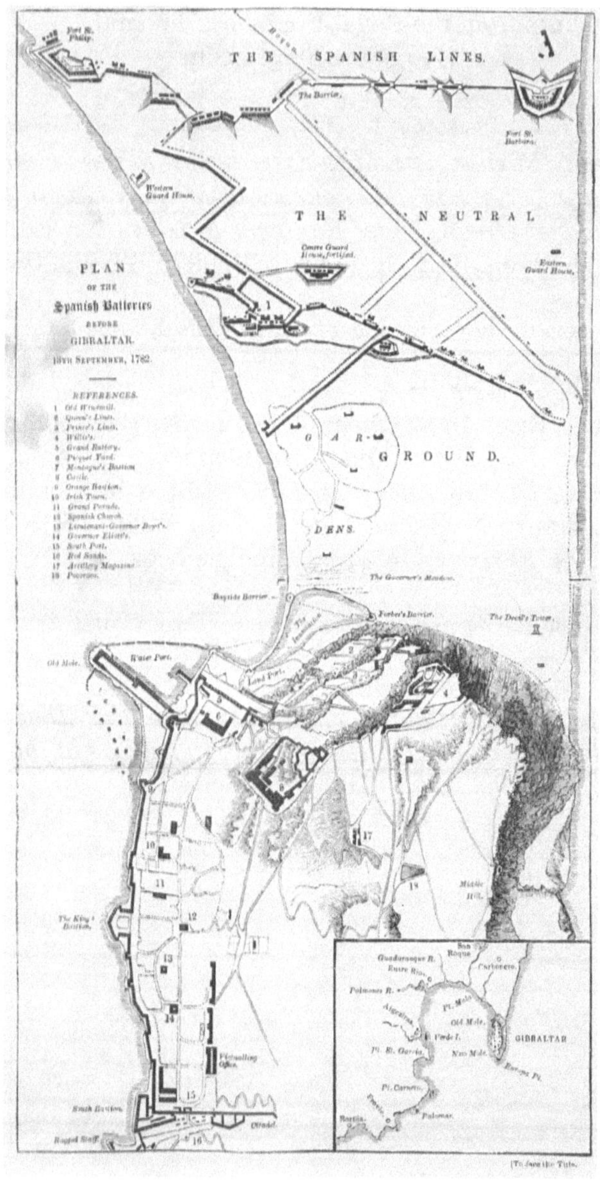

A map from *The History of the Siege of Gibraltar* by John Drinkwater.
London: John Murray, 1844

A Lady's Experiences
IN THE
GREAT SIEGE OF GIBRALTAR
(1779-83)

The Journal of Miriam Green, wife of Lieut.-Colonel
Green, Chief Engineer of Gibraltar

Edited by Col. E. R. Kenyon, R.E.

First published in the Royal Engineers Journal, 1912

2024
Waterville, Maine
pagesofpages.com

Table of Contents

Preface

This diary begins with descriptions of several social events involving both the British offices at Gibraltar and their Spanish neighbors. The siege seemed to begin gradually, but by the end of July, 1779, Mrs. Green wrote:

> [...] it is not be doubted but the Intention of the Spainiards is to attack this Garrison. I shall therefore from this time call then · *The Enemy* · whenever I have occasion to speak of them, which I shall do as long as Circumstances enable me to continue this Unconnected, Rough, Journal · and much I fear I should fall Short of any Stile or method, were it intended for any Persons Information except such of my Family Friends who perhaps will not Dislike to pass an Idle hour in looking over these pages. God only knows who may have the Sight of this Book or who may ever See the Person who now writes this; however I go on; *Miriam Green.*

The diary is one of several primary sources on life at Gibraltar during the siege that lasted from June, 1779 to February, 1883. Readers of her journal will find that her health was never very good, and she in fact left Gibraltar, for health reasons, returning to England in July of 1781. Her last journal entry was June 13th. She died a year later. Her husband, William Green, Chief Engineer at Gibraltar, survived her · promoted to Major General during the siege, was made a baronet, and in 1786 was appointed Chief Engineer of Great Britain. He died in 1811.

The diary was first published in 1912, over seven issues of the *Royal Engineers Journal*. The sections from each issue are presented as chapters in this edition. The history of the manuscript is described in the beginning of Chapter I, by the editor Col E. R. Kenyon. Kenyon was also a Chief Engineer at Gibraltar. In spite of not yet being published, the diary is quoted extensively by Whitworth Porter in his *History of the Corps of Royal Engineers* (Chapter V) published in 1889.

A History of the Late Siege of Gibraltar, 1779–1783 (London, 1785) by John Drinkwater is the standard early account of the siege. It had numerous editions and was republished into the 20th century. Drinkwater was a young officer with the 72nd Regiment of Foot at Gibraltar during the siege.

Another early source is *A circumstantial journal of the long and tedious blockade and siege of Gibraltar, from the 12th of September, 1779 (the day the garrison opened their batteries against the Spaniards) to the 23d day of February, 1783*, by Samuel Ancell (Liverpool, 1784). This was reprinted several times, with some variations in the title.

Another journal, not published until the 20th century, is *A Journal of the Siege of Gibraltar, 1779-1783* (Gibraltar, 1908) by John Spilsbury, Captain in the 12th regiment.

This is the third in a series of reprints from the Royal Engineers Journal of lengthy articles of significant historical interest that did not have a contemporary book publication · perhaps because of the onset of the first world war. The other titles are listed at the beginning of this volume.

A LADY'S EXPERIENCES IN THE GREAT SIEGE OF GIBRALTAR (1779-83).

BEING THE DIARY FROM 1ST JUNE, 1779, TO 13TH JUNE, 1781, OF MRS. GREEN, THE WIFE OF LIEUT.-COLONEL GREEN, CHIEF ENGINEER OF GIBRALTAR (AFTERWARDS LIEUT.-GENERAL SIR WILLIAM GREEN, BART., CHIEF ENGINEER OF GREAT BRITAIN, 1786—1802).

THE MS. of this diary, which has never before been printed, is the property of Major-General O. H. Nicolls, late R.A., the great-grandson of Sir William and Mrs. Green, who has very kindly allowed it now to be published. Except for the occasional correction of an obvious mistake in spelling and for the somewhat free revision of punctuation (of which, however, the general characteristics are preserved as far as possible) the MS. is reproduced *verbatim et literatim*, a very few private lines only being omitted and also a detailed private account of the illness and death of a maidservant from small-pox. There being two versions of the greater part of the diary,—both written by Mrs. Green—much of this reproduction is a compilation from the two. The original language has been everywhere preserved but the two versions have been blended together where necessary in order not to omit any fact or comment included in either of them. The diary is not only of interest as giving a lady's experiences of the Siege which has hitherto been only described from the soldier's point of view, but also throws additional light on the trials borne by the garrison and the military events of the Siege. For instance, although Drinkwater and Spilsbury both mention the slight outbreak of small-pox in October, 1779, they make no allusion to the much more serious outbreak which looms so largely in Mrs. Green's diary from 15th January, 1780, to 15th July and which carried off some 500 people, chiefly children, including about 50 soldiers.

Sir William Green whose mother was a daughter of Adam Smith, author of *The Wealth of Nations*, obtained his first appointment in the Corps of Engineers on 12th March, 1744, as Practitioner Engineer. On 14th May, 1757, military rank was granted to the Corps and he was then commissioned as captain-lieutenant. He served at Fontenoy in 1745 and under Wolfe at the capture of Quebec in 1759, when he was wounded, and in 1760 was sent as a major to Gibraltar to command the Engineers and to fortify the place, or rather to bring its fortifications up to date. In 1762 he was promoted to lieutenant-colonel; and in 1772 the

1

Company of Military Artificers which afterwards developed into the rank and file of the Royal Engineers, was formed on his recommendation. During the great siege of 1779—1783 he was promoted to the rank of major-general. He was created a Baronet in 1783 as a reward for his services during the Siege ; and from 1786 to 1802 he was Chief Engineer of Great Britain. He retired in 1802 and died in 1811. During the Siege his official quarter was approximately on the site of that which is still the Chief Engineer's Quarter, but he also had a private residence " Mount Pleasant " which he had built for himself outside the town and Mrs. Green's diary shows that both houses were used by them during the first two years of the Siege, and that at both of them bombproofs were constructed for use by the family whenever the enemy should bombard. At the " Mount,"— now the official residence of the Senior Naval Officer,—one of these shelters still remains and is used as a reservoir. It is possible that some of the underground tanks at Engineer House may have been formed out of Green's bombproofs, but the house was " entirely destroyed at the commencement of the enemy's fire from their batteries upon the Isthmus,"* *i.e.* in the bombardment of April, 1781. " The Mount" was sold by Green to the Admiralty in 1797, and the present residence on that site was built between that year and 1811, being considerably altered in 1846 and again enlarged in 1905. The baronetcy expired with Sir William Green's son, Lieut.-Colonel Sir Justly Green, who commanded the 1st Royals and was afterwards Military Preceptor to H.R.H. the Duke of Kent, father of Queen Victoria.

Mrs. Green was the eldest daughter of Colonel Justly Watson of the Corps of Engineers and grand-daughter of Lieut.-Colonel Jonas Watson, R.A., Chief Bombardier of England, who was killed at the Siege of Carthagena in 1741, aged 78. She died on 21st June, 1782, in England,† from the effects of a chill caught in the bomb-proofs in which she had to shelter in Gibraltar.‡

A few Mem relating to what passed in the Garrison of Gibraltar ; during the Investment, and Blockade which commenced upon the 21st of June 1779—and a few Mem* of what had passed, about 3 weeks before it happened, by which it may be seen how Unexpected such an Investment was to the English in Gibraltar. To make this more clear I shall begin with the first of June.*

1779.

June Tues 1st. I was Then very ill, Confined to my room, and found it would be impossible for me to go to the Ensuing Birth

* W.D. Bill Book No. 228 at the Record Office.
† Porter's *History of the R.E.*, Vol. I., p. 107.
‡ *Dictionary of National Bibliography.* Article on Sir W. Green.

Night ; for which there was great preparations making, and I learn that our Govr had been out himself to Invite the Spainish Govr of St Roque, Don Joaⁱⁿ Mendoza and his Lady and all the Spainish officers to come In upon the 4th of June, which shew'd all was Well at that time ; My Complaints Still remain bad,—all the 2nd, 3rd, and indeed for the rest of the month.

4*th*. Great bustle in the Garrison. The Field officers and Staff, all at Dinner at the Convent. At Noon there was as Many Guns as the King was years old. In the afternoon the Spainish Gov^{rs} Lady and Several officers came in ; but not the Govr himself, At Sunset there was a feu-de-joye. Madame Mendoza went from the Line wall, where she had seen the Firing, to the Convent ; where there was a very Grand Gala, a Ball ; and the Inside Court Yard, all round the Colonade, was finely Illuminated, and all possible pains taken on the occasion.

From the 4*th to the* 15*th* I continued greatly indisposed, and in my Room most of the time ; all this time things were very quiet, and Several of the officers and their Familys had gone out to St Roque, and in that Neighbourhood to stay for the rest of the Summer.

On Saturday the 19*th* the Govr and all the Colonels and Field officers of this Garrison were desired by the Govr to attend him in a Visit He made to Don Joaquin Mendoza, the Govr of St Roque, upon hearing of his having been promoted to the Rank of Lieut Genl. They formed a large Cavalcade, It was a very Warm Day. N.B. They returned to dinner. It was remarked that He did not receive This Visit as He ought to have done ; but Seemed Uneasy the whole time they staid—which was not very long—as He did not even ask them to Partake of any Refreshment ; and which indeed They ought to have had ready for our Govr &c, as they knew of his intended Visit. By what so soon happend, We can not help thinking that He had Rec^d some private hints, and in all likelihood was distress't at this Visit, Madame was there. The Party all came back in good Spirits, tho not much pleased. They all dined at the Convent.

Sun^d 20. I am much better and went to Church. Many people Riding out into Spain, and all quiet.

Mond^y 21. The Mail went out to St Roque as Usual, but We had not any come In ! which We did not mind at first, as it is not Uncommon for the Mail to stay an hour later than common. However we soon learnt the occasion. In the afternoon as some of our English officers were Riding out they were inform'd by the Spainish officers at the Lines that they must not go through, Not only that but that all the officers and families who were out were orderd into the Garrison directly, and also every English Person, not even allowing them to bring away those Necessarys they had taken out with them. Mr Davies and Family were there, also Mr Booth and Family, Capt and Mrs Montgomery, of the 12th, and Several others,

<table>
<tr><td style="vertical-align:top; width:20%">21st June, 1779.</td><td>With great difficulty the Spainish Govr allowed them to stay that one Night, but by 3 oclock He hurried Them away. From that hour all communication was shut up. At this time Colonel Ross and Captain Vinogles of the 39th was in Spain upon a Tour, and at Malaga when they heard of this. They Set off directly and arrived at St Roque on Wednesday the 23rd, but was not suffer'd to come into this Garrison ! the Govr Assuring them it was not posible for him to let any Body come into Gib^r They were thus obliged to go to Cadiz. There they staid some time, till an answere was returned from Madrid. They were then allowed to go anywhere but to this Garrison. They went to Farro,* From thence they got a Boat, and arrived at Gib^r upon the 25 July, as well as did Capt Lafanue of the 56th who had got as far as Lisbon by means of a Convoy, Under Capt Allen, of the Chatham Man of War, who sailed out upon the very Morning of the 25th before it was known of our Communication being Stopt. It is not impossible but Mendoza waited on purpose to let them be saild first, before He sent In Word, as He has a full View of all that passes in this Bay. Capt Lafanue left all the Convoy at Lisbon, but that the Levant Frigate, Captain Murry, was gone home express. I think his going was owing to the first Paquet Boat, which went from this, which was upon Tuesday 29th June to Farro, by which I wrote to My Sister and to Capt Nicolls,†—and thus ended this month. Only I am to remark that a vast Number of Ships and Xebeques‡ were daily going over to Algezira, and from them Several Smaller Vessels went to the Orange Grove.</td></tr>
</table>

July began very quiet. I was tolerably well and in pretty easy Spirits, tho' at times We had our Fears particularly as our Admiral did not seem overforward to let any of our Ships go out to stop any Thing that was daily going over the Way. Several Persons in the Garrison Seem'd Inclined to Man Vessels by way of Privatters. In the beginning of this Month 3 Fine Cutters came In from Engl^d fitted out as Privateers to take either French or Americans. They were stout Vessels indeed.

Sun^d 11th. I went out to the Mount. Several Large Ships appeared round Europa, and at Noon made Signals to the Admiral, who sent out the *Childers* Sloop of War. She found it was a large Number of Xebeques and other arm'd Vessels. A pretty Smart Engagement began, between the *Childers* and the 3 Cutters. It was from them as they were out cruizing that the Signals were made. They took Several Small Prizes of wine &c. It was now Eagerly

---

* A small port on the south coast of Portugal, frequently mentioned in this Journal, being the nearest neutral European port.

† Husband of Mrs. Green's eldest daughter, afterwards General Oliver Nicholls. He was in the 1st Royals.

‡ A small sailing vessel.

wishd and expected that the Admiral and the only Frigate viz. the 11th July, *Enterprize*, Sir Thomas Rich, would hasten out, as it was pretty 1779. certain this was a fleet intended for Algezira. At last Admiral Duff did make a Signal. The *Enterprize* got ready as Soon as possible, but it was 5 oclock before the Admiral got out. It was by much too late ! and the Fleet got through that Night. This occasioned great discontent and in consequence some Vowes &c were made.

Fri^d 16. Two Line of Battle Ships, of 74 Guns each, went over to Algezira, from which time it may be reckon'd a fair Blockade, as it can hardly be expected that any Vessel will be allow'd to come into the Bay.—We hear that the Fleet over the Way is to be under the Command of Don Antonio Barcelo, and it is well known that He is a Brave officer.

Sun^d 18. At Mount Pleasant. The whole Garrison seems displeased and Uneasy. Not any Vessels of late has come from Barbary, and our live stock is but little.

Mon^{ty} 19. The Colonel does not Seem to like our Situation at this time, and has order'd many things in the publick Way, and also inform'd me that He thinks it will be Necessary to be attentive to our having a good Quaintity of Useful Family things laid In. This Even^g I was taken with a Cold Shivering like an Ague ; and think I shall go to Town. Mr Logie, the English Consul, went over to Barbary.

Tues^{dy} 20. The Colonel came out pretty Early, and inform'd me that the Garrison was this Morning put under an allowance of Fresh Meat ! Each Corps is to draw in Proportion to their Number and the officers to have their Proportion, in Consequence our share came to two pounds, six ounces. N.B. This was what was allowed us to buy at the Common Market. He seemed so Very Uneasy, and said He was so much hurried, and at the same time not Well, that I was resolved not to Remain out any longer, as I thought I might be of Some little Use in Town at such a time as this. It was this Day reported that Mr Logie was taken in going over—(but it was not true, as We heard afterwards). The Vessel was Certainly Boarded by the Spainiards, and he was in the Dress of a Moor, not only So but hid himself under some Sails, and by that Means escaped. Otherwise He would most likely have been taken either to Ceuta or to Algezira.

Wed^y 21. I came into Town and find things a little better. A Boat had arrived from Tangier with 48 Bullocks. The Col. now seemed greatly indisposed, and upon Sunday 25 was so much that Doctor Baynes* advised him to be attentive to himself. This afternoon it was observed that the Spainiards had pitched one Tent near to Fort Negro.

---

* Surgeon-Major Arthur Baines.

26th July,
1779.

Mon^d 26. The Col had been much indisposed, and restless all Night. I really believe his Anxiety made him Worse. This Morning We saw a good Number of Tents pitched upon the Plains, or the Common, of St Roque, forming Several Streets. It now becomes Necessary to attend to every point, as it is not to be doubted but the Intention of the Spainiards is to attack this Garrison. I shall therefore from this time call them—*The Enemy*—whenever I have occasion to speak of them, which I shall do as long as Circumstances enable me to continue this Unconnected, Rough, Journal— and much I fear I should fall Short of any Stile or Method, were it intended for any Persons Information except such of my Family Friends who perhaps will not Dislike to pass an Idle hour in looking over these pages. God only knows who may have the Sight of this Book or who may ever See the Person who now writes this ; however I go on ; *Miriam Green.*

Tues 27. This day a Pacquet Boat went to Farro by which I wrote to my Sister. The Col still indisposed. Many Persons calling ; and the Govr expressing great Uneasiness at the Col's indisposition.

Wed 28. This day the Enemy encreasing their Encampment and making great Preparation. In the Forenoon the Govr came to our House and had a very long Conversation, and fixed many points with the Colonel. He also appointed the Staff of the Garrison, and fix'd upon his aid-de-camps, also many other matters, advising the Colonel not to attempt Stirring out till he was quite Well, as his Health now became a publick Concern. All this time and to the End of this month the Enemy continued very Busy indeed. Several of the Inhabitants families gat away by order and some indeed from Inclination. Inhabitants were order'd to Lay In for six months at Least. I now began to Fear upon the whole.

The Staff of the Garrison was settled as follows

Aid de Camps to the Governor, Captain Vallotton, 56th Regt, Captain Paterson, Royal Artillery, Captain Evelegh, Engineers, Captain Forch, 12th Regt.

Aid de Camps to Lt Governor,* Captain Wilson, 39th Regt, Lt Buckeridge, 39th Regt.

Aid de Camp to Lt Genl La Motte,† Captain Wenzee, Lt Gen La Motte's.

The Brigade Major to Hanoverians, Captain Lowder, Hardenbergh's.

Adjutant Genl Major Horsburgh, 39th ; Quarter Master Gen Major Hardy, 56th.

Town Major, Captn Burke, 58th.

Assistant Engineers, Lt Burton, Royal Artillery ; Lt Chambre, 56th ; Lt Att, 72nd ; Lt Schants, Hardenbergh's.

---

* Lieut.-General Robert Boyd.

† Commander of the Hanoverian Brigade which consisted of La Motte's, Hardenburg's, and Reden's regiments.

Mr Evans, Draughtsman to Chief Engineer; Mr Tingling, Draughtsman to Chief Engineer.

28th July, 1779.

Director of the Hospitals, Doctor Baynes; and Several additional Overseers in the King's Works.

The Colonel also appointed Lt Holloway* of the Engineers to attend upon him in some particular Dutys, which obliges him to have one officer constantly about him; and He became one of our Family.

The Colonel got better now every Day. From this time the Garrison was in constant Bustle, and in getting every thing in the best order. The Enemy also making very great Preparations, Unloading Stores, Pitching more Tents, &c, &c, and Thus ended the month of July. Various were the opinions; tho' it Seemed most probable that the Enemy's Intentions were to make every possible and effectual Trial to Establish a stronger Blockade, nor were they Idle to keep that Spirit up, as No one Vessel appear'd, either from the East or West, that Barcelo did not try to Stop, and most times with Success, He must be allowed every praise due to a good officer, altho' an Enemy.

August 1. The beginning afforded no very Essential Matter. Not any Vessels came over from Barbary. We now Endeavoured to Lay In as good a Stock as possible, and all sorts of family Articles were Sought for and Laid In. It is to be remark'd how very greatly the Inhabitants that kept little shops used to impose upon any Body. Nor were the Merchants backward in that respect! and most things were now fifty pr cent dearer than before.

Sun^d 8th. Miss Wards left Gibraltar in a Swedish ship, also Miss Hardy. I wrote to my Son and to Helen. This Day Lt Skinner of the Engineers declared his Marriage. All pretty quiet.

Tues ^d 10. I wrote to my Sister by a pacquet Boat by Farro.

27th. I wrote to my Son by a pacquet Boat, but it did not Sail till the first of Septr. Nothing happend particular the rest of this Month. It now became quite fashionable to get all the News each one could Collect; and by Way of Gaining all that, every Body was Using Spy Glasses from Morning to Night. All those that *affected* great *Cleverness* were ever ready with a pencil and paper, and it was realy Laughable enough to see with what a Jealous Eye each Aid de Camp look'd at the other, fearing *He* should be the first to communicate his *Ideas* of what He supposed the Enemy was about! Various therefore was the Reports, and could not always agree. Those remarks I have made (Such as I could not possibly make from my own Personal Observation) I think may be depended upon as they are from our own Corps, and mostly from the Gentleman that is in the Colonel's family, who would hardly bring a false account.

* Afterwards Major-General Sir Charles Holloway.

1st September,
1779.

*September 1st. Wed*ʸ· Easterly wind, exceedingly Warm and Close. Hear that the pacquet Boat had sailed for Farro in the course of last Night, and that those Vessels which were in Sight last Night were gone through. N.B. At this time the camp had not made any Material alteration for some Days, excepting two more Laboratory Tents, making 5 in all.

*Thur*ᵈ *2d.* Westerly wind. At one this Morning it rained exceedingly hard for half an hour, the first rain this Season. We all expected it would be Worse as at this time of the year it is often very Violent, but it turn'd out a pleasant Morning and forenoon. We this Day Laid In Several family Matters. No change in Camp this Day. Beef very bad at Market, and only 3 Bullocks to be killd, and those very Dear.

Fry 3rd. Westerly wind. Fine Morning. The Spainiards busy in Unloading Stores at the Orange Grove ; and every Morning and Evening they bring down from that Landing place and from Fort Negro, Large Quaintitys of Stores in Carts, likewise many Cannon may be Seen from our Upper Batterys. Great complaints are now making in the Garrison for Want of fresh Provisions, not any Beef or Mutton in the Market to Day. Inhabitants, particularly Jews, are Laying In provisions for Six Months.

*Sat*ʸ *4.* Westerly wind, pleasant Morning. A pacquet Boat arrived from Farro, last from Tangier, brought 10 Sheep only ! An other Regt came to the Camp this morning. Some few persons had letters from England, but none from our Friends. No meat in Market Mid-Day had Soup Meagre for the first time.

*Sun*ᵈ *5th.* Westerly wind. Exceedingly Close and Damp. No Boats would Venture over to Barbary upon account of the Spainish cruisers. A man of the Hanoverians deserted this morning, was fired at from Williss. The wind came Easterly in Evening.

*Mon*ᵈ *6th.* Easterly wind. The Same Close Damp Weather. This Evening a Boat went to Tangier in which Several Inhabitants went over. Amongst the Number were Mr Butler, Dutch Consul, and his Niece. I wrote by this opportunity to My Daughter Nicolls. The Same Movements in the Camp. Most people now begin to think *We* ought to take Some Notice of our Neighbours, as they continue to *Work* on very Briskly ; and are very Busy at Fort Negro, Fort St Philip and Fort Barbara.* Our *Admiral* and his Small Squadron remain perfectly quiet. Many Town Vessels go out and are very active !

(To be continued).

---

* St. Philip was on the west, and Barbara on the east, flank of the Spanish lines, the ruins of which still remain on the Spanish frontier.

A LADY'S EXPERIENCES IN THE GREAT SIEGE OF GIBRALTAR (1779–83).

Being the Diary from 1st June, 1779, to 13th June, 1781, of Mrs. Green, the Wife of Lieut.-Colonel Green, Chief Engineer of Gibraltar (afterwards Lieut.-General Sir William Green, Bart., Chief Engineer of Great Britain, 1786—1802).

(Continued).

Tues^d 7th. Westerly wind. Cold, Damp, and Uncomfortable. In the Evening there was Some Fire Balls, Other Experiments from the South Bastion, and from the *Enterprise* Frigate. Blows hard at Bed time and all Night. 7th September, 1779.

Wed^y 8th. Easterly wind. The Same Close Weather. The Enemy very Busy at Fort St Philip, bringing down from their Camp large quaintitys of Stores ; some Mortars also, &c. We this Day carried up a twenty four pounder up to the North Lodgment.

Thur^d 9th. Easterly wind. It rained exceeding hard this forenoon. It must have given the Enemy a good weting. It cleared up in afternoon. Their Tents appear very wet.

Fry^d 10. Easterly wind. Our People very Busy at the New Battery above the North Bastion. It seems now to gain Credit that our Govr intends to Fire upon the Enemy Soon. The Govr is at our House this and every other Day for this last Month, but no one can tell the Result of these Meetings, as there is never any one Present, except himself and Colonel Green. I am now following the example of a good Many of the Inhabitants &c, sending some of my most Valuable Furniture and other Matters out to the South. Many of the Jews and others have obtained leave to erect small Houses, or rather Hutts, at the Southward. I have also Divided our Stores and Live Stock between this House and the Mount, as it may be very likely I and the Female part of our Family, will be Under the Necessity of being out there, in case the Enemy should Fire upon the North part of the Garrison.

Sat^urd 11. Easterly wind. Hear there is to be a Council of War at the Governor's this forenoon, Consisting of the three Colonels and the Admiral, as follows—The Governor, General Eliott—Lt Govr Lt Genl Boyd—Lt Gen La Motte, Hanoverians—Colonel Ross, 39th Regt—Colonel Green, Chief Engineer—Colonel Godwin, Royal Artillery—Admiral Duff—Captain Sir Thomas Birch.

Various now were people's opinions. However it was all silent. In the Evening Genl Boyd was here for two hours with the Colonel.

The Evening passed as Usual, and the Col ordered his Horses at Gun Fire the next Morning, as indeed He does almost every Morning. Every Body in the Garrison has given up all Sort of Entertaining, as Early hours at Night as well as Morning was now become Necessary, nor were the Days passed without great hurry of business. I am now coming to a very Interesting part, and will Endeavour to be as particular as I can, in order to make it Understood in a Small degree how we were all Circumstanced at this Time. Several officers were under the Necessity of keeping Journals. The Engineers all do for the Chief Engineer's Inspection, and *He* keeps a very Separate one, which I believe is not intended to be shown to any one in this Garrison. My few remarks are as I said only for my Family.

Sun^d 12. This Morning at half past Six the Garrison began to Fire upon the Enemy. The first shot was from the New Battery call'd the *Superior*,* above the North Lodgment, 900 feet high. It was fired by Captn Loyd, Royal Artillery. We kept up a very heavy Cannonading for an hour. Most of the Garrison got upon the Hill. I never heard such a Noise in my Life. It is impossible to express the Bustle of the place. I mean amongst the Inhabitants. As to the Troops all was quiet, or as other Days. No Soldiers were allowed to go up the Mountain but those on Duty. The Govr was up as high as Williss. There was most of the officers, particularly The Artillery. There had not any Orders been given on that Head, as that would have made the business too publick ; Indeed I believe it was not known to Ten persons including the Council. I can safely say I had not the least Idea of it, any further than it was Universally believed We should begin in a Day or two as We all thought it was to Commence as Soon as Ever the Chief Engineer had Reported the New Batterys being ready, and He had thrown out hints of that being about the following Tuesday or Wednesday. To return now to our Morning's business. The Colonel returned to Breakfast at 9. From that time the firing keep up all the Day from the North parts of the Rock, more or less, as our People discover'd the least appearance of any of the Enemy's Troops. In the afternoon there were Six Mortars fired, 2 of the Shells fell into Fort Barbara. We keep it up till 11 at Night. An easterly wind all the Day.

It is not easy to describe the hurry that this Days business Involved every body in, as it was Supposed the Enemy would Soon Answer our *Salutes*. I have already mentioned that many of the Shop keepers were removing their Goods &c. Great quaintitys were already gone ; and this Day made them truly Anxious to remove what was still left. For this business every Person had full Imployment— Porters running here and there—old and young Jews frightened to Death almost as their *Dreads* greatly exceed all other Degrees of People. By the Night near all the North End of the Town was

* Afterwards named *Green's Lodge.* See 13th inst.

totaly abandon'd, The officers were likewise trying to change Quarters, particularly such as had families. I did not move any of my family, only as I mentioned before, sent off every chief part of my most Valuable Goods. Our plate was put into a Boomb Proof, my Household Linen, Books, and Cloathes, to Store houses at the South End of the Town, and our Stock as I before said, at the Mount, leaving only real and Useful Necessaries in the Town Quarter (which is quite in the Line of Fire). During this whole Day we could easily distinguish the hurry the Enemies Camp was In, When the First Shott was Fired they were relieving the Guards at the Lines, and at the same time Large Parties were employ'd bringing down quaintitys of Stores, as Usual, in large Waggons and Carts, drawn by Horses and Mules. I saw Several myself, whose drivers had left the poor Horses &c standing, whilst They made off, We know that Several Mules and Horses were killd. The Colonel has order'd a Boombproof to be made in the lower part of our Gardens at Mount Pleasant. It was a Reservoir for Water and is about 15 Feet long, 10 Feet broad. It will be a very good and Comfortable Consideration in Case of an attack by Sea, and if that does not happen it will keep the Water always cool in case we wish to Turn into the original Intention. It appears as if it would be a very Good Place.* [12th September, 1779.]

Mond^y 13. Easterly wind. The Enemy had been heard at Work all the last Night and the Garrison had fired 6 shott in the course of the Night, and again early in the Morning. At 10 oclock I went out to the Mount to see how the things were disposed of there. A very fine day. I staid till Even^g' heard Various reports of what We had done by our yesterdays Work, The Govr has given the Name of Green's Lodge to the highest Battery newly Erected which had taken the Name of Superior. It is a Work now found to be of a very Essential consequence, and was at first proposed to the Govr before the least Idea of the Communication being stopt, even as March last, by Colonel Green. The Govr submitted it to him, and it was begun about † weeks agoe.

Tues^d 14. Easterly wind. The Enemy not at all advanc'd. Very few shott sent last Night. The Colonel all over the Mountain to Day. The Garrison in good Spirits, Towards the Evening the wind seem'd Westerly. One thirteen Inch Mortar fired this afternoon. Uncertain of the Effect. We are sending to the Mount more things to Day.

Wed^y 15. Easterly wind. The Enemy much the Same, and our firing rather less. Several flying reports of our having kill'd Men as well as Horses the other Day.

---

* It is still used as a reservoir, but the original roof was removed about 1907 to allow the lawn tennis court to be extended.

† The figure here has been corrected and is very doubtful, but appears to be a 3 or a 5. It was actually commenced on August 20, 1779.

16th September, 1779.

Thurs^d 16. Easterly wind. The Garrison keeping up a smart firing all the forenoon, on account of Working parties. In the afternoon We fired three Shells from a thirteen Inch Sea Mortar, pointed from our upper heights, towards the Laboratory Tents. The two first Burst as Soon as fir'd and fell into the Sea. The third went into the Camp, within 400 yards of the Tent in Front. It has afforded Us Satisfaction in General as we now are getting the Range of our Shott &c. It is to be tried again. N.B. The Mortars are found good but not the Shells.

Fry^d 17. Easterly wind. Very Close and Hot. I find myself growing much indisposed. So much hurry has affected me. More Tents are pitched in the Enemy's Camp. There are 13 Battalions now come, and it is said there are to be 16 in all. There has been only one Working party seen to Day. It is Supposed they are a little Alarm'd at what passed on the 12th and yesterday, and as it is conjectured have sent off an express to Madrid. I have omitted to mention in Due place that the Streets in the Garrison were begun to be plowed up on Tuesday the 14th inst. They began in Irish Town, and plowed up the Main Street to the Grand Parade. This Day They are in our Street and have come up within a 100 yards of Us.

Satur^d 18. Easterly wind. The Enemy the Same ; We also keep up a Smart firing as of late. At Noon it began to Blow Westerly, and a Venetian Ship got In, bound for Holland. I grew much indisposed, which gives me great Concern at this time.

Sun^d 19. Easterly wind. I had been in great pain all Night in one Foot particularly, and proposed Staying in bed all Day. However upon hearing that the above Mentioned Vessel was going to Sea this Day, I used every endeavour to write home and would not on any account mention the painful Situation I was then In. I wrote to My Sister and inform'd her that We had been very *Noisy* and Busy ever since this Day Week. We had Several Gentlemen to Dine this Day, and in the afternoon the Colonel was obliged to go out at Landport to make *Observations*. He went as far as the Gardens ! with only an *Orderly* Sergeant, as it was not proper to take any Number ! I was uneasy till He came back. A Shell was Fired this afternoon with good success at Fort St Philip. In the Course of last week—about Friday—the Cupola of the White Convent* was taken down also the Arch and upper part of the Governor's Church.† All the Inhabitants and Shop keepers in the Main Street from Bedlam Barracks down to Waterport have left their houses. At 8 this evening a great Number of Shells and Shot were fired. It surprised most people, what could occasion so Much Firing. Captn Johnson upon the Batterys.

---

* Probably the Whitefriars Monastery which was at this time the Admiral's residence. The site is now occupied by Bland's Stores.

† The King's Chapel.

Mond 20th.   Easterly wind.   The captain of the Batterys began 20th September, 1779. to Fire as soon as Day appeard and fired an amazing Number of Shells, so much that it is allowed He could not have kept up a heavier fire had the Enemy been at the Gates.   This conduct is disapproved of. Major Lewis* relieved him this morning.   N.B.   This is the first Day that the Major has fallen In to do the Duty of Captain since He had the Brevet Rank of Major.   The Enemy has made some few advances, and have taken down some Stone Centry Boxes, likewise the Roofs of some Guard Rooms.   In the Evening we threw some Shells, with good Success it is said, into Fort St Philip.   Hear that Poca Roca cave is fitting up in high order for the Reception of the Governor.† The Venetian did not go last Night.   Find myself a little Easier to-day.   Every kind of Provision now is exceedingly dear and scarce.

Tuesd 21st.   Easterly wind.   A great Number of Shot and Shells fir'd this morning.   Nothing to be had at the Market except one Hog which is Sold at 3 Rials‡ per pound, equal to fifteen pence Sterling. Captn Eyre upon Batterys.   Very Moderate in firing all Day and Evening.   The Weather exceedingly Hott now.   My foot better.

Wed^v 22.   Easterly wind.   At half past 12 last Night we had a Number of shot fir'd.   It continued for near a quarter of an hour, and again a few more Early in Morning.   Capt Grove went upon Batterys this Morning.   The Enemy have made some additional alterations in their camp, and Several Rows of Tents are pitch'd towards the Eastern Shore, in a line from the first Tents.   Our firing very Moderate all Day ; a few Shells at 10 at Night.   We have taken no Notice of this day, viz., the Coronation Day.

Thur 23.   Easterly Wind, fine Day.   One other Tent, a Laboratory one it seems, Under the Queen of Spain's Chair, and likewise an Additional Number to the Left Line.   Capt. Loyd upon the Battery to Day.   Very Moderate in firing all Day.   More Tents in evening. Find that most of the Regts are come to the Camp except one Battalion of the Catalonians.

Fry^dy 24.   Westerly wind.   Little Firing this Morning.   Hear the Enemy has made More advancement in their Lines, and also that 2 Mortars are at the Lines.   This piece of News is doubted by some. Capt Paterson upon the Batterys to Day.

Satur^d 25.   Westerly wind.   No Firing all Night.   Capt Sowerby upon the Batterys to Day.   In the afternoon we fired 6 Shells from Green's Lodge ; five and half Inch Shells, out of a twenty four pounder.

---

* This officer was in command of the Artillery at the end of the siege, having succeeded Lieut.-Colonel Tovey who died on 27th November, 1781, and who had himself succeeded Colonel Godwin.

† It was never taken into use by him.

‡ Capt. Spilsbury in his diary gives the following monetary table :— 1 Dollar is 8 Reals ; 1 Real 16 Quarts ; 1 Pistol, 5 D. 5 R. ; 1 Cob 12 Reals ; 1 Doubloon 22½ D.   The Dollar at 42 pence sterling makes the Real worth 5¼ pence.

4 went into Fort Barbara, one into the Sea, the other Burst. Two Bullocks, belonging to the King's Works, are to be killed for to Morrow; which are by the Chief Engineer's orders to be Sold at a Rial and half. All the beef that has been of late were sold at 3 Rials pr lb.

Sun^d 26. Westerly wind. Very little Firing last Night. Capt. Johnson upon Batterys this Day. The Enemy preparing for Enlarging their Camp. This Day at Noon a Soldier of the 72nd, employed as a Carpenter out at Landport, went off the Works and got to one of the Hutts; was fired at from Williss with Grape Shott and also Some Shells; and Some Shott went into the very Hutt. The Man was not seen at all. It is therefore Uncertain whether this man is killed or remains there, to get off in the Night. This afternoon a Dutch Vessel was coming In. The Enemy's Row Galleys and Boats took Her when she was very near our Admiral and carried her over to Algezira. This whole Day the Spainish Admiral has had a Red Flag Hoisted upon his Main Top. They examined the Dutch Vessel and then let her go. A Top Sail Vessel appear'd from the East this Even.

Mond^y 27. Westerly wind. The Spainish Admiral has the Same Red Flag hoisted this day. This Morning a Swedish Vessel taken. Supposed to be the one that was in Sight last Night. She was also Carried over to Algezira. She Saluted the Spainish Admiral with 7 guns who returned 3. Major Lewis upon Batterys.

Tues^d 28. Westerly wind. No material alteration in the Camp. The Spainish Admiral has the same Red Flagg for the third Day.

Wed 29. Westerly wind. The Enemy are getting Mortars upon the Point, Fort Negro. Capt Martin upon the Batterys. The Spainish Admiral has not the Red Flagg this Day. It is conjectured it has been owing to a Court Martial held on board. Very little Firing this Morning. Mr Holloway came down at Noon from the Midshipman's lookout and reports that He has very clearly seen 4 Mortars Mounted at Fort Negro. He Saw Some of them as they were bringing from the Orange Grove, drawn by 20 Mules each Mortar. There has orders been given this day for the Steeple of the Spainish Church to come down, and the Clock and The Bells likewise.. This Evening was cold and damp. Great Complaints for want of Fresh Provision.

Thur^d 30th. Westerly wind. Colonel went up to Williss. Capt Grove upon the Batterys. The Mortars are removed from Fort Negro and taken to the Lines. This is a cool Morning, and at Noon it appeared like Rain. There was some Veal in the Market which was Sold at 5 Rials, 2 Shillings of English money, pr pound. This Even at Sun Set, when the Enemy fired their Evening Gun as Usual at Point Negro there was a Ball in the Cannon. It was Seen by Many as it fell into the Sea. It is supposed to have been owing to their having Neglected to take out the Ball in the Day time, as they always Used to do. We have been very Moderate in the Firing this 30th September, 1779. Day.

October 1st. Fry^d. Westerly wind. This Day the Guards mounted at 8 oclock. Capt Loyd at the Batterys. We have keep up a Smartt firing this Morning. Writing a letter to my Son to go by the Venetian Ship which was to have gone upon the 20th of last month.

Satur^d 2. Westerly wind. Colonel went up to Rock Guard. Capt Sowerby upon the Batterys. Very little firing this Morning. The Enemy are Unroofing a Guard Room at the Lines. N.B. It is to be remarked that We have been very attentive in one point, which is that of never having fired any one Shott at the officers Guard Rooms. It has in general been directed to the Working parties, &c. It rained a little this Day and Blows fresh in Evening which gives Us hopes of Boats coming over from Barbary.

Sun^d 3. Westerly wind. In the Night it began to Rain pretty hard attended with Thunder. At Guard Mounting it came on very hard. Capt Johnson upon the Batterys. The Govr has order'd that there should not be any 13 Inch Mortars fired to Day. At Noon it Cleared up and the Wind came to the East. Several Shott in afternoon. The Enemy have brought down a Mortar to the Artillery Park. The Venetian sailed this aftrnoon. It rained all the Evening very hard.

Mon^d 4th. Easterly wind. A man of the 58th Deserted last Night from Middle Hill Guard. This makes 5 that have deserted since the Investment, three Hanoverians, one of the 72nd and this of the 58th. The Enemy have lighted up Fires in their Camp to air Themselves after the Rains. Major Lewis upon the Batterys to Day. The Enemy have added 2 more Laboratory Tents in the Artillery Park, one in the Front, the other in the Rear.

Tues^d 5th. Westerly wind. Raining very fast. Captn Eyre upon Batterys to Day, Very little Firing. The man who Deserted Yesterday was found this forenoon, quite Dead and most of his Limbs Broke to pieces.

Wed^y 6th. Westerly wind. Captain Martin upon Batterys to Day. The Enemy has brought down 2 More Mortars to the Artillery Park. A few shott fired to Day. In the Evening We had a Signal up for a fleet.

Thur^d 7. Westerly wind. Fine Morning. Col. went to the South and to New Mole. Capt Patterson upon the Batterys.

Fry^d 8. Easterly wind. Capt Loyd upon Batterys. A French Privatter took a Swedish Vessel as she was coming In and carried her over to Algezira. Our Artillery People are very Busy this Day Taking a twenty four pounder up to the Rock Guard which is an amazing height ! and of course a very difficult Business. The bomb proof at Mount Pleasant is now Completed, only wants Airing. It is a very Comfortable looking place.

Satur^d 9th. Westerly wind. Fine Morning. The Colonel at the

9th October, 1779. Castle before Breakfast. About 10 this Morning a firing began in the Bay, between some Spainish Row Boats and some Xebeques, and the *Childers* Sloop of War, who was going out to protect some of our Men of Wars Boats who had taken a Prize and was bringing it In. They were fired upon; a chace ensued and it obliged the Sloop to return to her Station after having been out about an hour in which time she had got up nearly as far as the Orange Grove and had been fired at from Fort Negro. Admiral Barcelo, &c, and all the Camp had Turn'd out Under Arms. Captain Paterson upon the Batterys. This forenoon a Circumstance happened in the Bay, besides what I have just mentioned, that gave great displeasure to the Garrison, viz., a Boat from Barbary loaded with Bullocks was going over to Algezira about the time of the Sloop being out in the Bay. It is Supposed that We might have brought Her Into the Mole with Ease, had our Frigate gone out. All this adds to the discontent of every Body, and many very Disagreable things were said on the Occasion, and some of the officers of the Navy and Army behaved in a Slighting Manner to Admiral Duff Who carried it with an Air of Indifference!

Sund 10. Easterly wind. A very fine Morning. Colonel upon the Rock. Breakfasted with Captain Sowerby who had the Batterys to Day. Very moderate in the Firing all day.

Mond 11*th*. Easterly wind. A Dull Day. Major Lewis upon the Batterys. The Enemy Seem busy upon the Common about 100 yards from the Strand, between the two Guard Rooms. They are employ'd throwing up Some kind of Work. They have about 150 Men at Work.

Tues 12. Easterly wind. At the Castle before Breakfast. Captain Eyres upon Battery. Two Town Boats for Cattle sailed last night, one of which was pressed by a Spainish Vessel, which obliged the Towns People to quit Her, and take to a Smaller Boat. They took our Vessel and Carried Her over to Algezira. The other got safe to Tangier. Very little firing all Day.

Wed 13. Easterly Wind. Capt Martin upon Batterys. The Colonel went up the Hill at 10 oclock to see the Gun Fired from the Rock Guard, attended by Capt Loyd who Laid the Gun. They Fired at the Western Fort. Most of the Shott took place and greatly alarmed a Party of Dragoons who at first took it to be the Blasting of the Rock, till such times as they found the Shott amongst them! They then made into a Ditch.

Thurs 14. Westerly wind. Captain Patterson upon Batterys. The Colonel at the Castle before Breakfast. Last Night a Hanoverian Captn Belonging to La Motte's Died Suddenly. A man of the 58th trying to Escape from Middle Hill was Dash'd to pieces. At this time I was Taken exceedingly ill and continued so till the End of the year. I shall not therefore be able to put down any Daily occurrence. However the most Essential I shall Endeavour to set

16

down Here, as I was just Enabled to put a few Interesting Circum- 14th October, stances into my pocket Book; which makes me able to carry on a 1779. Sort of Journal; at least of what was Most Material.

On the *27th* of this month I wrote to my Sister by a Venetian ship which did not sail (till) the 2ᵈ of Novᵇʳ· I was not able to keep up any Journal. Nor did any very Interesting or Essential change or Difference in our Situation occur. Every Article of Provision had long been too Dear and too Difficult to get. This had made it a very Uncomfortable Circumstance to every one in the place. However upon the whole the Troops keep up a very great degree of Spirits. Nor ought I to omit Saying that the Governor took every Necessary Means to take care of them and their Families, Endeavouring by every method to oblige them to Lay In as much fresh Dry Stock as it was possible for them to get ; and therefore every officer help'd their men and at least to answere for them. However the poor Inhabitants began to look in a very Uncomfortable Way ; the Jews in Particular.

*November 1st.**

11*th. Thurs*ᵈʸ· The two first Deserters came In, of the Wolona Guards.†

*Sun*ᵈʸ 14. This morning a fine Cutter was chased into the Bay by the Spainish Men of War. She got to Windward of the Enemy and drove the Spainish Admiral &c behind the Hill. She proved to be a Folkestone Privatter called the *Buck*, Captain Fagg. He Brought Her In with the Utmost Conduct as a Sea Man and with Spirit. From this time the Enemy's Fleet was dispersed and left *US* Sole Masters of the Bay ; it was therefore expected that *We* should have availed ourselves of it. However it did not turn out So ! As our Men of War made no attempt to move. All this Seeming Neglect hurt Every Individual in the Garrison ; and Several very Severe Papers were put up on the Different Parades Reflecting upon the Admiral's Conduct. A Windmill was now Erected up the Hill, near the Garrison Hospital, in order to Grind the Wheat that was taken from a Dutchman. Many of the Inhabitants in much want. The Chief Distress is the Want of Flour and of Firing—two very great Wants indeed.

about *the 20th.* The Enemy took Two Neutral Ships in the Face of the Garrison and very near to the English Admiral, and one of them was a Swedish Vessel Loaded for this place belonging to some Jew Merchants, who inform'd the Admiral it was the Vessel they expected as she made the proper Signals, but He did not chuse to send out any assistance ! by which We had the Mortification to see her taken over to Algezira, and We Were deprived of Many Articles this Garrison stood in great need of, particularly Coals as the owners

---

* No entry follows this date.
† The Walloon Guards.

20th November, 1779.

were certain there was a Large quaintity on board. About this time Mr Holliday, the principal Baker in this Garrison, refused to Bake, owing to the want of Wood. He had at this time 51 Sacks of Flour left. The Gov' took them all away except two which He allowed him to keep for his Family. In the beginning of this Month the Small Pox first Broke out in the Garrison. It began in an Inhabitant's House, a poor Jew's. One child was nearly Recovered before it was found out, and an other taken ill. Every Method is taken to prevent the disorder spreading, as it would have been a very bad thing at this time. The Means were used as follows—an examination was made amongst the Different Reg^{ts} of those Men who had not had the Small Pox, and they were directly orderd out to the Southward, and the same Number Sent In to do the Duty; the Jew's family was removed to a House in Irish Town; a Large airy place. They were ordered to be keep close and to admit of none to those who went In with them. As other children were taken ill, they also were sent to that House; by which means it avoided Spreading. There was 7 Children in all that had it, but it never took amongst the Troops. I shall observe when the Troops were brought back to their Respective Reg^{ts.}

Upon the 27th of Dec^{br} the Small Pox being all over the Troops were all properly fix'd—the children still kept in Irish Town—and no communication whatever with the rest of their Relations. It is not certain how this Disorder got into the Garrison. Some think it was brought In by some Privatters' Men who were taken out of an English Ship which run on shore near Fort Barbara, which ship was Burnt.

December 1st. In the beginning of this Month the Weather was very Mild and pleasant. I went to the Mount for a week.

10th. I wrote to my Sister, sent it by a Packet Boat to Barbary. I was taken ill about the Middle of this Month and came to Town. It began to be very bad Weather; and also the Garrison had all the appearance of having a very bad Season in all Respects coming on. The Troops were Well and as yet in good spirits, but the great Want of Flour and of Firing began to oppress. The Boat which had gone over upon the 10th to Barbary came back a few Days before Christmass and brought a very few Goats and fowls which sold at an amazing Price. There was some very bad Beef, old Cows, to be kill'd against this Holiday time—(as it used to be call'd)—but so bad and so very Dear that it could not be thought of (but) by very few indeed. It now Rained every Day.

Christmass. This Day was tolerably fine as to the Weather, and every Body tryd to appear Easy and Contented. We had a few Friends to dine with Us, and upon the whole we did the Best We could.

Sund 26. Raining and Unpleasant Weather. The Enemy quiet just now; many of their Tents are unpitching, and it is rather at this time an *Hutment* than an Encampment of Tents. We Seem to 26th December, 1779. Understand by Several More Deserters that They are in nearly as Much Want as ourselves.

Mond^y 27. The Enemy this forenoon Fired 4 shott, supposed to be at our Fisher Men who had indeed gone too near the Spainish Coast. One of the shott, a twenty four pounder, went into the Head of the Princes Lines, but did no harm. It Blowed very hard all this Day and the next Night ; but to let us See how Unexpectedly the Goodness of Providence is at Such times as We poor shortsighted Mortals think ourselves in the utmost Danger, behold in the course of this last 24 hours We had a Blessed supply of Wood which had been brought down to the shore near to the Ruins*, intended for the Use of the Camp. It was chiefly Brush Wood. The wind Drove directly into the Bay. The same fortunate wind Drove it towards the New Mole ; and it was going round towards Europa. Our Men of War sent out their Boats. They got a Large Quaintity,— and what Ever We could stop, that was done near the Old Mole and outside Landport. It was a great Supply for this Garrison, as it is at the least calculated to amount to 500 Quintals and will be enough to Supply the poor Inhabitants and Soldiers Families for Six Weeks. The Govr gave those men leave to get into the Garrison who had families. It was Truly a God Send and highly Worthy to be Remembered, and it was likewise a Loss to the Enemy. Just before Christmass Day the Bakers left off Baking. We then began to Use our own Stock of Flour. We first began by taking 10 lbs of Flour and making into three Loaves, Sending Wood to the ovens (the Bakers having none). Our Flour was exceeding White and Good ; there was now remaining some of the Kings flour in the Victualling office which We the second time try'd and mix'd with some of our own ; it made tolerable Bread. N.B. This was flour from the wheat Ship that was taken from on board a Dutch Man some Months agoe. Several Deserters had come In from the time the two first came, which was upon the 11th Nov^br and they all report that the Camp was very Sickly and ill provided, and that the Enemy frequently come out from the Lines and go to the Gardens of Landport and Rob. I have as yet omitted to mention that upon the 14th of this Month a Spainish Deserter of the Wolona Guards trying to Escape to Us was fired upon from Fort St Philip, and a Party of Horse came out from their Lines to take him. He was hurt by their shott and likewise received a Wound from one of the Horse Men, was taken back into the Camp and the Next Day was hanged upon a very high Gallows Erected upon a high Hill, and left hanging all Day. By the Boat from Barbary we find all Communication between that Part and Portugal is totally

---

° The ruins of Carteia appear to be meant. Drinkwater says the wood was washed down from the banks of the Palmones and Guadaranque. Spilsbury says about 5 tons were collected.

Stop'd.   The last Venetian was took.   The Boat which went over to Barbary upon the 10th Inst return'd as I have before said a few Days before Christmass and brought a very Small Supply.   I shall now proceed to mention the astonishing Price of Family Articles upon the Close of this Year, but first I am to observe that whenever any of the Oxen belonging, and employ'd by the Chief Engineer, in the King's Works, was ordered to be Kill'd for the Supply of the Troops and of the Garrison—(which was done as the Grain and Straw was drawing near an End)—this Beef tho' exceeding Fatt and Good was by the Chief Engineer's orders sold at 2 Rials per lb.   All other beef tho' not fitt for eating hardly for 4 Rials.   The Boat brought a few Goats which sold at 18 Dollars a piece, equal to £2: 15: 0.   At other times 6 or 7 Dollars was looked upon (as) rather Dear.   They are cheap in Barbary.   The Fowls, very bad, sold at one Doll' 4 Rials. We had not any Mutton in the Market for a long time past; till the Day before Christmass when one very bad poor sheep was Kill'd !— which was Sold by the Quarter at Eleven Dollars two Rials pr Quarter, equal to Six and thirty Shillings Sterling.   I can not avoid Mentioning a Circumstance which happened to our family During the Blockade ; One Day I had a Leg of Pork brought home from the Market ; it was very good Meat, but it absolutely cost nine Dollars, equal to one pound 10 shillings ! what a Sum for one Joint of Meat ! and at that time if I had not bought it no other kind of Fresh Meat presented itself—only think of the Poor.

The Prices of Meat & Poultry at the Close of the Year 1779.

			D.	R.	Q.		£	s.	d.
Beef per lb	...	...	0.	4.	0.	...	0.	1.	9.
Veal per lb	...	...	1.	0.	0.	...	0.	3.	6.
Pork	„	...	...	0.	6.	0.	...	0.	2.	6.
Goat	„	...	...	0.	6.	0.	...	0.	2.	6.
Flour	„	...	...	0.	2.	0.	...	0.	0.	10½.
Pease	„	...	...	0.	1.	0.	...	0.	0.	5.

The above shows the high rais'd price in English as well as in Spainish.   As to Poultry it was not very Easy to fix a price, as any one which had to dispose of any strove to get the most for them. However it was in General as follows.   N.B. I had no occasion to buy, having most exceeding plentyfull Fowl Yards, at a very great expense indeed, but still I had enough.

		D.	R.	Q.		£	s.	d.
Turkey, a piece	...	18.	0.	0.	...	3.	0.	0.
Geese	„	...	9.	0.	0.	...	1.	10.	0.
Fowls	„	...	2.	0.	0.	...	0.	7.	0.
Ducks	„	...	3.	0.	0.	...	0.	10.	6.
Pigeons, a pair	...	1.	4.	0.	...	0.	5.	0.

and when ever we got Fish it was beyond all Price.

(To be continued).

A LADY'S EXPERIENCES IN THE GREAT SIEGE OF GIBRALTAR (*1779–83*).

BEING THE DIARY FROM 1ST JUNE, 1779, TO 13TH JUNE, 1781, OF MRS. GREEN, THE WIFE OF LIEUT.-COLONEL GREEN, CHIEF ENGINEER OF GIBRALTAR (AFTERWARDS LIEUT.-GENERAL SIR WILLIAM GREEN, BART., CHIEF ENGINEER OF GREAT BRITAIN, 1786—1802).

(*Continued*).

NOTE.—From 1st January, 1780, until 15th January, 1781, there are two versions of the Journal, both in Mrs. Green's handwriting, but not identical. Frequently they are word for word the same, but sometimes one and sometimes the other has additions, omissions, or slight variations of language. Perhaps both were prepared from a rough original, such as the pocket book referred to in the entry following October 14th, 1799, or the one in two volumes (commencing on June 1st, 1779) may be the original, while the other (in one volume, commencing January 1st, 1780) may be the transcript referred to on February 2nd, 1780. The following is therefore a compilation from these two MSS. :—

1780.

Saturday. January the First. 1780. Easterly wind. Cold Morning. The Govr did not receive any Compliments in Form. He was as Usual upon the Grand Parade. We had only 8 Friends at dinner by Way of keeping up an Old Custom ; the Times were too bad to allow any family to entertain ; not only that but I was greatly indisposed and totally out of Spirits. The two Spainish Frigates went from Algezira. A Vessel in the course of last Night went to Cork. Several Persons call'd as Usual this forenoon ; but not near so many as on former Occasions, indeed most people now began to look rather Unhappy at our Uncomfortable Situation. The Troops are in good Health and Spirits, and have been so during the whole Blockade.

Sun^d 2. Easterly Wind. A Dull Cold Morning. We call this with good Reason the *Coolest* New Year that was ever experienced in Gibraltar. Find myself not quite so lame or ill as I was yesterday.

Mond^y 3. Easterly wind. Began raining just at Guard Mounting. The Enemy Seem Busily employ'd in covering themselves from the Wet. Their whole Camp seems under Water. We heard they are Sickly. Admiral Barcelo remains quiet over at Algezira with some Xebeques.

1st January,
1780.

Tues^d 4th. Westerly wind. Tolerable looking Morning. Col and Mr Holloway dined at Capt Loyd's. Find myself a little better.

Wed^y 5th. Easterly wind. Col dined at the Convent, not Mr Holloway. The Enemy the same way employ'd. Many Tents taken down and very large Hutts erected. No firing now. A General Court Martial ordered for to Morrow to Try a Soldier of the 58th for Theft. Two Deserters came In from the Wolona Guards Infantry.

Thursd 6th. Easterly wind. Cold Day. The man who was Try'd yesterday is Sentenced to be Hang'd. No firing today.

Fry^d 7th. Easterly wind. Had company to Day—all Gentlemen. The man is to Suffer on Monday next. He is and has been an old offender. The Troops are a little inclin'd to Break out at this Season.

Sat 8th. Westerly Wind. Very Dull Morning. It began to Rain in the forenoon ; Continued to do So all Day. At Noon came into the Mole a Vessel from the East brought to by the Guns at Europa— a Neapolitan loaded with Barley—said to be intended for Spain ; it is supposed the Govr will detain the Barley for this Garrison ; it is looked upon as a very great Blessing at this time, as it will help the poor Inhabitants and the Soldiers Families who now begin to Want.

Sun^d 9th. Westerly wind. Clear Morning, but soon began to Rain ; and at Guard Mounting it was Violent. Continued bad the whole Day. The Man of 58th would not go to Church ; or even allow our Clergyman to go to him !

Mon^d 10th. Westerly wind. It left off raining in the course of the Night ; and it was a clear fine Morning. The Man went out at South Port at 11 oclock, the Usual Ceremonys being observed. The Party was Commanded by Lt Col Cochrane of the 58th Regt. The man appeared perfectly Stupid and had refused to have any Clergyman till at the very hour of his Suffering. He then allowed of the Prayers that our Clergyman offer'd to read for him ; but said he was a Quaker, had deserved Death on Many former occasions he said,— an Irishman. This Day at Noon 5 Ships of the Line went through to the East, supposed to be part of D'Estaing's Fleet from Cadiz. The Ship which seemed to belong to the Commodore appeared to be Under Jury Masts. This Day turn'd out pretty fair. The Enemy appear Busy at their New Raised Batterys upon the Sea Coast, of which they now have nearly completed 3. They now seem to shew as if they intended to act upon the Offensive as well as Defensive. Barcelo's Ship is Closer into the shore than it has already been, and there are people who say He is Unloading part of his Stores and some of his Guns. However it is so Much the Stile to say every thing that Sounds like *Information* that I never depend on anything that I hear except form our Corps, who have good *Reasons* for all they Say.

Tues^d 11.   Westerly wind.   Fine Day but Cold.   About 3 oclock
in afternoon the Enemy Fired 4 Shott towards the Garrison from
Fort St Philip, supposed to get the Range.   One Shott fell into the
Gardens, another into the Governor's Meadow, and one into the
Inundation, the other not known.   There was a Funeral Party going
out at the time, and as the Burying Ground is very near to where the
Shot fell it greatly alarmed Them.   They only Staid to put the
Corpse hastily into the ground and the Clergyman &c hastened back,
since which no Soldier or Inhabitants are to go out to Landport to be
Bury'd.   A place is to be appointed out at Southport, near to the Jews
Burying place.*   The Working Partys and the Mules were all order'd In
directly.   Captain Sowerby was upon the Batterys and Fired from
Williss.   We were Engaged to pass this Evening at Capt Evelegh's.   I
own I was half afraid.   A large party.   We passed a very cheerful
Evening.   One of their youngest children appeared not very Well.
All Remaining very quiet.   A very fine clear Night.

Wed^y 12.   Westerly wind; fine Morning.   At half past 8 the
Enemy Fired 2 Shott; one a twenty four pounder; the other Grape
Shott, which Grazed the Battery at Water Port.   The other (viz., the
Grape Shott) fell between Bay Side and the Glacis.   At half past 10
they Fired 3 Shott from Fort St Philip, one of which Grazed a
Centry Box and went into the Spur Guard at Landport.   It was supposed that this was meant for the Flagg Staff as there was a great
Many of our Artillery officers there.   They also hurt a Mule who
was in a Working Cart.   The Colonel was looking over the Ramp at
Landport when this happened; and one of the twenty four pounders
fell within 3 feet of him!   The third Shott came into the Town and
fell upon the Roof of an Inhabitants House in a Back Lane in
a Line with the Spainish Church—(there was not any Persons
living in the House, they having Quitted it and gone into Spain upon
the first of the Troubles).   A Woman who keeps a Milliners Shop
happened to be going by at the same time; had her Leg struck by
some part of the Splinters of the Roof or by some of the Shell Work
out of the front of the house.   She was thrown down and insisted upon
it both at that time and since that it was the Ball that hitt her Leg.
However that was impossible as it must have broke her Leg.   She
was more alarm'd than any real hurt.   It put Us all into a sort of
Bustle and the same kind of Fears took hold of the Jews as did upon
the 12th of September.   Some of the Shopkeepers had taken away
their Goods upon that Sunday's Firing, but as they found all had
remained so long quiet they had about a Month agoe begun to bring
them back to their Shops!   So They now began to hurry them away

---

* Drinkwater says "A part of the Red Sands behind the Princess of
Wales's Lines was appropriated to that purpose."   The "Lady Augusta's
Battery" is a part of those Lines; so that this is probably the origin of
the Sand Pits Cemetery.

12th January, 1780. for the Second Time. Indeed it now look'd to be more Necessary than at the first, for it was now most reasonable to expect the Enemy would come on. I had a further supply of Family Matters sent to the Mount, but as the Weather was cold I did not Stir myself. I sent the child out this Day.

Thurs^d 13. Westerly wind; it began to Rain very early, and continued to do so all Day. Everything quiet from the Enemy, but the Garrison in a Bustle. Much talk at this time about the Provisions,—as it certainly must be nearly Reduced. Thundered in Even.

Fry^d 14th. Westerly wind, raining at Guard Mounting. Colonel Ross of the 39th came out to the Parade this morning for the first time since He was so very ill, which was in the Month of October. He called upon us after Breakfast. Had a Meeting of Colonels and Field officers at his quarters in forenoon, relating to the Provisions for the Troops. Their allowance is to be in part Lower'd. It is from the Beef and Pork they have been obliged to Reduce this. We hope that by this Regulation there is remaining in the office enough for 3 Months. The Troops all Seem Satisfied and are in good Health and Spirits. Some few Friends in the Evening. This Evening a Man of the Artillery, Capt Loyd's Company, was Drownded at the New Mole. He was in Liquor and fell off a Plank. I was taken ill again in the course of the Evening, a Cold Shivering and a pain in my Left Arm.

Sat^y 15th. Westerly wind; Raining all Morning. Find myself exceedingly ill; pains all over. Doctor Baynes call'd in the forenoon and greatly alarmed me, by telling Us of the Small Pox being again Broke out, upon a Child of Captn Evelegh of the Corps of Engineers; this is a fine Boy, about Six Years old. He did not seem very Well when We sup'd there on last Tuesday Evening. They have two Younger to have this Disorder. It hurt me to hear of this: and also the whole Garrison as it is not a thing to be wished, just at such a Juncture as this, when we can only Manage People in Health. We were in hopes that by the great care that was taken in Nov^{br} last and by every appearance at the close of the year that it was all over,—however it could not be so, as Undoubtedly this little Boy had taken it by having been at play with the Spainish and Jew Children after they had returned home. We hear that the Govr will not allow of any Innocculation. Whilst I was thinking of the Unpleasant Prospect that Presented itself and supposing everything that is bad would follow,—behold at 2 oclock we heard of a most Interesting piece of News ! A Vessel appear'd coming round Caberitta point, which proved to be an English Store Ship ! Oh ! What a Joyful Sight ! The Sloop of War was sent out, likewise the Cutters and Arm'd boats. They brought her into the New Mole—with more than half the Garrison looking at Her ! We find it to be a Brig, in the Ordnance Service, call'd the *Sophia*, bound for Minorca, with 3 Artillery officers for

24

that place. As Soon as the Admiral's Boats went on Board, we 15th January, heard three cheers, which was answered on board the *Admiral* &c., 1780. &c. We now hope for Good news, which, thank God we had. She brings information that she is one of a Grand Fleet coming to this Garrison, consisting of Three Admirals and 21 Sail of the Line and that one of the young Princes is on board the *Prince George*, Admiral Digby, that they all left Portsmouth upon Christmass Day, were separated five Days after they had left Eng^d , in a Gale of wind. This news you may be well assured was truely Welcome. We find there is a Post Chariott on board this Brig for Us, but that is a Mere Trifle in comparison to any one word of good News that is brought to this Garrison. The pleasing hopes of a happy relief to this place is too great to express. I strive all I can to get well and to partake of this happiness, but I grew so bad with my Left Arm in the Evening that I was almost Distracted. It Rain'd hard in the Evening. A man of the 58th Deserted this Morning. We are in Earnest expectations, laying for the next Day, in hopes some of the Convoy may be coming In, as the Master of this Vessel thinks they must be near at hand.

Sun^d 16. Westerly wind. Blowing and raining. We grow Uneasy about the Fleet. These 3 officers of Artillery are very Young Men, and They do not exactly agree in their Accounts, and for the most part say they do not know whether all, or only a part of the Convoy is for this place, or even who they all are. All this makes Us full of eager hopes and fears. I am a little Easier. A Spainish Deserter came In this forenoon, of the Wolona Guards. Nothing appeared all Day from the West! At last, about 7 in the Evening we heard some Signal Guns from our Admiral. They were made to a Vessel which was going up too high in the Bay. She was order'd into the New Mole, and proved to be a Ship belonging to Merchant Anderson, Loaded with Flour, and had left the Convoy 5 days agoe. She brings an account (this rather a Confused one) of an Engagement. Oh! how we all long'd for Morning to know more. It was blowing very hard. We had a Number of different Reports brought In between 7 oclock and Bed time. We hardly know what to think.

Mond^y 17. Westerly wind, very windy and. raining hard. Find myself still very bad, and my anxiety great. The Troops were this Day put upon a Shorter allowance, as to Beef and Pork. They still appear Satisfied. Capt Evelegh's Son very ill. At Noon it Blew a perfect Storm. Every one is Uneasy about the Fleet. No News all Day! Let any one Judge of our Anxiety,—but that is not possible, except by those who have experienced the like Circumstances. No Firing on either Side at this time. Barcelo still nearer the land.

Tues^d 18. Westerly wind, a more Moderate Morning. About 10 oclock a Joyful Sight presented! A Prize brought In, taken by

18th January, 1780. Some of our Convoy, a fine Rich Ship Loaded with Oil, Tobacco, Soap, and Bale Goods. At Noon a much larger and more Valuable one came In, a Prize to one of our Men of War. She was brought In by a Lieut of the Man of War who had taken Her, is Loaded with Brandy and Masts. Now We are certain of our Good News. There has been an Engagement indeed! The Particulars are not well known, any how We now expect more Ships. This is the Queen's Birthday, but no Notice is taken, any otherwise than by the Royal Standard being up. It began to Rain hard and to Thunder in the Evening. Several large Ships in Sight, and in the Close of the Day an English Frigate came In, which proved to be the *Apollo*, Capt Pownoll. He was greatly surprized when going on board the *Panther* to find that Admiral Duff was not on board at such a Juncture as this! but He was inform'd the Admiral was a *Quiet Man!*

Wed 19. Westerly wind; at Day Break our Governor ordered 21 Guns to be Fired into Fort Barbara, and the Royal Standard was up. At Guard Mounting the Admiral also hoisted the Royal Standard and Fired 21 Guns, the Drums all Beating, the Men of War giving 3 Cheers, and the Parole was "*Victory.*" The *Edgar*, 74 Guns, Capt Eliott, came In this Morning. She brings great and Glorious news; our Fleet in their passage first fell in with a Fleet of Carraco Ships, took 7 of them, Estimated at £400,000! sent them all except one to Eng^d. Then upon Sunday the 16th they fell in with part of the Spainish Fleet. They had a very hot Engagement off Cape St Vincent, a kind of running fight. The *Bedford* ran 80 miles during the Engagement! It Ended by our taking 7 of their Line of Battle, and one 80 Gun was Blown up; every Soul on board Lost except one poor Wretch who Died in a few Days. We took their Admiral, Don Juan Langara, in an 80 Gun Ship, the *Phœnix*. We hear the whole Fleet are expected In here. They consist of 21 Sail of the Line, besides Frigates. The whole place is now full of Joyful Confusion. I find myself Something better; and Even Strive to appear more so than I am in reality. We do not hear as yet of any Material hurt to our fleet. The Spainish Admiral is now coming In, on board his own Ship; a good deal wounded. He wished not to be removed from his Ship, and gave his Word to our Admirals that his Men should bring his Ship In Here, or any Port they chose. He was Trusted, and is now coming In. He has lost more than 200 men. It was to the *Edgar*, Capt Eliott, and the *Defence*, Capt Cranston, that the *Phœnix* struck. It Rained and Thundered all this Evening. Several Men of War coming In. This Evening Don Juan Langara was brought on Shore and taken in a Sedan Chair to a House prepared for his and his officers Reception. He was allowed to bring all his *Suite* and Baggage. He is not Mortally Wounded, but his first Captain is. We also hear that a very fine

Young Man in our Service has had his Leg Shott off, Lieut Forrest, ^{19th January,} on board the *Ajax*, and a Lieut of Marines Kill'd. No others as yet ^{1780.} that We hear of. Lt Forrest has a Brother ; a Lieut in the 58th Regt in Gibraltar.

Thurs^d 20. Westerly wind. Early in the Morning The *Prince George*, 90 Guns, Admiral Digby came In, on board of which was His Royal Highness Prince William Henry. The Royal Standard up in the Garrison for the third Day. The Prince came on shore at Noon, had no particular Honors paid him. He went to the Convent ; from thence He was attended by the Govr. the other Generals, and the Chief Engineer up the Hill as far as Williss. This is the King of Spain's Birth Day, and it has been said it is the Enemy's Intention to Fire upon this Day. Barcelo's ships are all Dress't, and He fir'd three times as is their Custom. He is Certainly Drawn Nearer the Shore ; and We See there is a Work going on over at Algezira. Some of his Guns are likewise taken out. More of our Fleet coming In, and several officers calling. The Highland Regt also are arrived. The Colonel was Taken not Very Well this Evening and fear He is going to be indisposed. We hear there is a great quaintity of Provisions and Stores come to the Garrison. All now is Joy and Bustle.

Fry^d 21. Westerly wind. More of the Convoy coming In. The Prince on Shore again, Walking about. He dined at the Convent. This Day at 3 oclock 6 officers belonging to a Spainish Man of War who was wrecked upon the Coast of Spain were allowed to pass into Spain, in order to Settle about Exchange of Prisoners. They went out with the Town Major and a Drum. No Firing from us Now. Several of our old acquaintances calling. Lt Trigge of the *Bedford* here in the Even^{g.} At 12 this Night we were all alarm'd by a Firing from the Enemy from the Forts near the Sea,—Point Negro, Fort St Philip, &c, Algezira. We naturally concluded it was now their Intention to begin, and I declare I did expect to see the Shells in the Town any moment ; it was now that I really was alarmed. It was at 4 of our Men of War which had come in, and by the Current was hurried up near to the Lines ; it alarm'd the Enemy more than Us, as no doubt they expected it was an attempt to set Fire to their camp. They fired an amazing Number of Balls and one Shell. It Wounded the Rigging of the *Terrible* which was one of the 4 ships and hurt a few Sailors, also one Spainish Sailor who was on board the *Terrible*. They all got back to the New Mole. It was a very fine Moonlight Night. The appearance of the Enemy's Firing was a Grand, tho' alarming Sight, and I own I suspected it was their full Intention to throw Some shells into the Town. Thank God they did not ; and we all went quietly into our Beds at 3 oclock. There was no Confusion or any Bustle in the Garrison ; the Picquets were out, as usual at these times,—and always are upon any particular firing.

22nd January, 1780.

Satur^d 22.   Westerly Wind ; a Cold Raw Day.   Many of the Convoy not as yet come In.   The Colonel was not better for having gone out in the Damp last Night, indeed he grew very ill in the Evening.   We got 2 English Sheep from our old Friend Admiral Digby.   This Morning more of the Small Pox appear'd, at an Inhabitant's house.   Capt Evelegh's 3 children are all Lay'd down in the Disorder.   He is obliged to leave his House for the time, not being able to stay from his Respective Duties at such a Busy Period as this.   No Persons are allowed to go to his or any Inhabitants Houses, except the Doctors.   The General will not allow of Innoculation as yet, but Says He will as soon as it gets amongst the Troops. This Day we get a Box of Things from on board one of the ordnance Ships which had been on board Six Months, consisting of Family Matters for myself and child.   Also We Receive 3 sheep and a cask of Butter from Mr Veale at Portsmouth.   The Colonel grows much Worse in the Even^g·   The *Nottingham* Store Ship, with Colonel Picton, Lt Col Craig, and Several others arrived this Day,—all hurry. Get some oranges as a Present from Capt Pownoll who has been over to Barbary.   We hear that Admiral Sir George Rodney is over there.   The *Childers* Sloop is cruizing about the Bay.

Sun 23.   A Dull Morning.   The Col: not worse.   Began to rain after Breakfast.   A good deal of company of the new comers &c this Day at Dinner.   This evening after orders,* relating to the Commanding Officers, to give In a Return of the Troops fit for Service, by which it is supposed that the Highland Regt is to be Left here. At 10 this Night the Colonel grew exceedingly bad.   It was a very Stormy Night.   The *Childers* Sloop of War that went out two days ago returned from Barbary with expresses from Sir G. Rodney who is over at Tetuan but will not Venture In till all the Convoy is Safe. We hear that the *Royal George* Admiral Sir J. Ross is behind the Hill.   This Day I experienced both pleasure and pain ; Joy for Good news ; and Vexation at the Colonel's Indisposition,—So very Unlucky.

Mon^d 24.   Westerly wind.   The Col very ill, did not get up till after dinner, obliged to send excuse to Admiral Digby for not being able to dine with the Prince today.   Great hurry and much Confusion in the Garrison, Unloading the Stores and Provisions ; every place towards the South is to be made use of for the King.   Get 4 Sheep from on board the *Nottingham*.

Tues^d 25.   The Colonel still very indifferent.   This Morning Admiral Sir George Rodney ·arrived in the Bay.   In the forenoon 5 of the Wolona Guards made an attempt to Desert from the Lines. They were followed close by a Party of Horse as far as the Gardens, and some even as far as our late Burying Ground.   There they killed one

---

* *i.e.* " After-Orders " were published.

Man and Mortally Wounded an other who died just as our People got 25th January, 1780. him into the Bayside Guard. The other 3 got safe into the Garrison. We fired both Grape and Round Shot at them from Williss, but did no other Execution than killing one Horse and hurting an other. In the Course of this afternoon most of the Convoy got In and also Sir John L. Ross. No sort of Supply of Fresh Stock as yet from Barbary, by which means the Garrison was as badly off as before ; only with this difference,—We were all in Spirits and had frequent presents of Mutton &c from our old acquaintances in the Fleet. This forenoon I received a Small Box from on board the *Nottingham*, Under Care of Lt Col Craig, Containing letters, papers, Books, &c,—our last dates 18th Dec^{br.} I was obliged to write Cards of excuse from the Colonel to Several Gentlemen who were to have dined here as to Morrow, he being too ill to See Company. Raining all this Evening. Have been writing this Evening to my Friends in England, and have begun to Transcribe from my long Journal a few Articles which I intend for my Son ; as I understand the Convoy may go Unexpectedly. Also I have begun some letters to go by the *Childers* Sloop which is to go the very first Instant the wind will allow.

Wed^y 26. Westerly wind, fine Morning ; the Colonel something better. At 8 oclock Capt Evelegh came to ask for two Mules to bring Sir G. Rodney from the Landing place, as he was expected to come on Shore, and the Govr had a Litter ready for him. The Prince on Shore today, but the Colonel could not attend upon him. Several Persons call'd. All in great hurry Still.

Thurs 27. Easterly wind. The Colonel still very Indifferent. Doctor Baynes thought it better to Bleed him. All Busy in the Fleet. Flaggs of Truce all day going about in the Bay, and Parleys from the Lines. We sent away the Sick and Wounded Prisoners. I finished one long letter to my Sister which Sir John Ross enclosed in his Pacquet. The Sloop expected to go to Night.

Fry 28. Easterly wind ; Raining and a bad Morning. The Sloop not yet gone. Several Promotions in the Navy. Capt Macbride is going home in the *Childers* Sloop with Dispatches. He has changed from his former ship the *Bienfaisant* to the Spainish Admiral's, the *Phœnix*. A Lt is to command in Capt Macbride's absence. Capt Conway has got the *Bienfaisant*, and Capt Peacock who had the *Childers*, has got one of the Large Spainish Prizes, called the *Diligenta*, and a Lt of the Admiral's (Sir G. Rodney) goes home in the Sloop, taking Capt Macbride as Express. This Day turn'd out exceedingly bad. Blowing and Raining very hard. The Colonel not Worse. We had two Hampers of Sugar brought on Shore this Day, which was on board the *Nottingham*. We Understand they were for us, being in the Bill of Lading, tho' the Directions were off. They are totally destroyed, and not one pound will ever be used in the house ; they are wet and have also been destroyed by all sort of Vermin. It is believed it was all owing to Carelessness. This is a Loss, but a greater disappointment than even the Value at such a time as this. This Day more Flaggs of Truce and Parleys. All Firing has ceased now. At 8 at Night it Blew exceedingly hard. The Sloop has attempted to get out but We are doubtful, as it Seems coming to the West. All this time Don Barcelo seems busily employ'd in getting out his Guns, and it is beyond a doubt that there is a Battery on the Shore near to Algezira. The Report is that the Camp is exceedingly out of Spirits, and Don J. Langara has declared to our Govr and Admirals that the French has deceived Them !

Sat 29. Westerly wind, Raining and Blowing a perfect Storm. The Sloop was obliged to return in the Course of the Night, after being forc'd to throw over 3 Guns. Lt Howe* of the 12th was the only officer of the Garrison allowed to go home ; and he was sent for from England upon account of his having got a Company in a new raised Regt. This forenoon a Spanish Frigate came from the West, most certainly a Stranger to what was in the Bay. She was chased by one of our Line of Battle and a Frigate, but Unluckily They were too Late. She got too close into the Shore. Our 2 Ships of War keep up a Smart Firing upon her, particularly the *Edgar* (the Line of Battle Ship). She (the *Edgar*) got under their Guns and all the Battys and Pigeons Island† &c, all fir'd. The Frigate seem'd greatly hurt by our firing ; and was Tow'd into Algezira by all the Boats from Barcelo in the Evening. A very bad evening. The Fleet for Minorca getting ready. Sir William Draper is going to his Lieut Government. It is Settled for the Highland Regt to remain here, and They are getting all ready at the Bomb proofs under the King's Bastion for their Reception, and at the Picquet Yard under the Grand Battery.

Sund 30. Westerly wind, raining exceeding hard all Night and this Morning. N.B. It is just now the very worst Weather we have had this Season, which is Unlucky as it in Some degree retards the publick business ; at least it makes it Uncomfortable to every Body, particularly those who are employ'd in Unloading Stores and Provisions. The Minorca Convoy sailed this Evening. The Colonel getting better every hour. Intended going out today but was persuaded to stay at home ; it turning out so wet. I finished a letter to my Son and gave it to Captain Macbride who expects to sail as soon as ever it is in the smallest degree favorable.

Mond 31. Westerly wind. Indifferent Morning. Col at Guard Mounting. The whole Morning but very Dull ; and the afternoon Still Worse. The Col sent cards for company on Friday next.

---

* Or How.

† Another name of *Green Island*, off Algeciras.

Flaggs of Truce all Day. 3 men of the Wolona Guards came In, 31st January, which makes 22 in all. They are to go on board our Fleet. The 1780. two first which came In (viz., 11 Nov^br) have remained in the Gov^rs Gardens at Work.

February 1st. Tues^d. Westerly wind and a very Dull Morning. Col at G. Mounting. It Thundered all Morning, poured with Rain all Day. The *Childers* got away last Night, but we fear is drove behind the Rock. Sir J. Ross call'd here. This Night turn'd out the worst We have as yet had,—Thunder, Rain, and Wind,—the Ships all driving about and Several Signal Guns firing. Every body is anxious for our friends in the Bay, and all long for Morning.

Wed 2nd. Westerly wind, bad weather still. Col better, dined with Col Ross and passed the Evening.* I am as busy as I can spare the time in Transcribing a Small Journal for my Son, but am frequently broke In upon, by the Number of Visitors that are constantly calling; Not only that but the Daily Necessity I have in attending to all sorts of Family business, makes it almost impossible to go on in the Writing Way. I shall at last get into a Total disregard to Method, Stile, or Sense I fear; for as I wish to write to the *Very Moment,* so it can never be the Effect of a Studied writer.

Thurs 3. Westerly wind, a very Wet bad Morning. The Colonel better and able to go to Parade; and out upon the Hill. The Prince did not come on Shore this Day, it turn'd out too bad. Very Busy this Day in Settling the Manner of Exchange of Prisoners. Barcelo is quite close In Shore; and it is now observed that There is a Boom making over at Algezira against Landing, such as ours at Water Port. We do suppose He is half afraid of our Men of War. There is also a Battery completed, near to Algezira.

Fry 4. Westerly wind; Raining Still. The Col kept waiting to See if the Prince would come, tho' it appear'd too bad; however at 12 He came, and the Colonel attended him upon the mountain. Flaggs of Truce in the Bay. We had a very Large Company, of the Navy chiefly, at Dinner. The Colonel returned very late to Dinner, exceedingly wet from his walk. He brings Word that the Admirals and the Prince would Breakfast at Mount Pleasant to Morrow. I accordingly order'd everything Proper; and mean to go myself if the Day will admit. A great deal of Company this Evening. Lt Forrest of the *Ajax,* who as I mentioned before was Unfortunately Wounded, and who had been brought on Shore Some Days to his Brother's Quarters, of the 58th Regt Died this evening, very much Regretted. He had got Promotion, Sir G. Rodney having just appointed him Master and Commander, in the hopes He would Recover. He was

---

* Here ends the entry for this date in the single-volume version of the diary, which renders it probable that it is the transcript referred to in the following sentences.

<table>
<tr><td>4th February,
1780.</td><td>just 20 years old; a very fine Young Man; Universally Esteemed. The *Childers* Sloop got through yesterday.*</td></tr>
</table>

Sat 5. Westerly wind; a clear and fine looking Morning, and luckily continued So all Day. It was the only tolerably pleasant one that has been since the Fleet came In. I went in my chair to the Mount. The Prince &c came on Shore about 9, and walked first to the Cave &c, the Colonel with him; and Ended the Walk at the Mount where everything was in proper Readiness. He was Delighted with the Gardens and Walks; it was favorable, so pleasant a Day. I was as much pleased with Him. He is a very fine Youth and must be liked in any Situation. His Questions were proper; they all wore the face of being the Result of a proper Curiosity. After the walk was over the Colonel went on board the *Prince George* to Dinner, and I return'd to Town that Evening, very well Satisfied with the Day.

Sun^d 6. Cold Indifferent Morning. The Col: busy in writing till Dinner at General Boyd's. This Day Capt Robinson in the *Shrewsbury* arrived to the Satisfaction of Many; that Ship and the *Dublin* being mis'd. The last is obliged to Remain at Lisbon to be made fit to go to Sea. The *Shrewsbury* has taken a tolerable prize; and Sold Her at Lisbon. Neither She nor the *Dublin* were in the Engagement upon the 16th Jan, having been Separated in a Gale of Wind before that Day. Sir J. Ross here today.

Mond 7. Westerly wind. Busy writing for the Fleet as it is expected They will soon leave Us. We have a very large Party at dinner this Day, Sir J. Ross and many of our Navy Acquaintances; and also of the Highland Regt. In the forenoon the Colonel went on board the *Sandwich*, and gave an invitation to Sir G. Rodney to go to the Mount as He has expressed a wish to Lay a few Nights on Shore. Sir J. Ross has pressed me exceedingly to go on board the *Royal George* and to take a Rough Dinner with him on Wednesday; also to take my own Party, all which I have promised to do, tho' at the Same time, think it will not be possible; as it is very likely the Wind may be Easterly; in which case I Understand it is likely that Division may have orders for Sailing. I should very well like to see so fine a Ship, particularly as Sir John is so pleasing and so cheerful an old Man. A very large Party at Night. N.B. Colonel Ross quite in Spirits now his Friend is here. We all wish, for his own sake, He could go home with the Admiral.

Tues 8. Westerly wind. The Colonel out all the Morning with the Prince and Admiral Digby &c. The Fleet in a hurry. At noon I heard that some part of the Fleet was to sail directly. I employ'd most of the forenoon in getting Journal and all *Writings* ready, tho' as I observed before, it is no Easy Matter to gain the time; as it

---

* "This Day" in the two-volume version.

32

is quite impossible to be *Denied*, our Situation will not allow it ; our House is Constantly full. I find it rather too much for my Strength or Spirits but can not help it. The young gentlemen very Busy in the Plan way. 8th February, 1780.

Wed 9. Easterly wind, fine morning, but think I shall not be able to go on board ship to Day, as Some of the Ships seem getting Ready. At 11 a Signal gun was Fired from Sir G. Rodney for Admiral Ross and his Division to go to Sea directly. I received a Message of excuse from Sir John, and they were off before one oclock. This Day Don Juan Langara received an express from Madrid, informing him of the King having appointed him a Rear Admiral, with the Rank of Lieut General. N.B. He was only before Brigadiére de Marina. We send off some more Spainish officers and Sailors in a Flagg of Truce. N.B. We have not had any in return yet. Mr Raleigh, the Gov^{rs} Sec^{ry} is appointed Commissary for Exchange of Prisoners, and goes at all times in the Flag of Truce Vessels. Many of the Spainish Sailors are mortally Wounded.

Thurs 10. Easterly wind. It is now Settled that the Spainish Admiral is to go back into Spain in consequence of letters which has passed between our Admiral in Chief and the Court of Spain.

I have omitted to mention that Admiral Duff went on board the *Royal George* on Saturday last with an Intention not to come on Shore any more. He goes home as Passenger with Sir J. Ross. There was no Ceremony Used at his going. He call'd upon a few Persons only. We were of the Number. He seem'd a good deal discomposed and Disconcerted.

Fry 11. Easterly wind. All Bustle in the Garrison. Unloading ships and getting ready for the Fleet. The Colonel every moment employ'd. Many Parleys every Day, and letters from the Commander in Chief in the Camp, Don Martin Alvares, and our Governor, and between Marquès Gonzales de Castejon, Secretario de Estado y del Despacho de Marina, and Admiral Sir George Rodney. Don J. Langara dined this Day on board Sir G. Rodney, as did the Prince &c. Don J. Langara is to go away in two Days. N.B. He had dined at the Convent before and was exceedingly politely Received. He was highly pleased with the Young Prince ; and made him a Number of Genteel Speeches. He spoke in French, which His R.H. speaks very well.

Saturd 12. Easterly wind. The Prince took leave of Me and was again at the Mount. They talk of sailing either to Night or in the Morning. All Bustle, all Confusion. My letters going by different Hands. The Colonel Dines on board Sir G. Rodney, finds the Store Ships will not be able to go, it being impossible to get Ready. This Day the Spainish Admiral went away. Great Civility shown him. He went in a Vis-a-Vis of the Gen^{ls.} was drove quite close to the Gate at the Spainish Lines. Several officers attended him to our out

12th February, 1780. Guards, but no further; only as Usual the Town Major and one Drum as with a Parley. Great Compliments at parting, and a very great Cavalcade meet the Spainish Admiral with Led Horses &c at the Lines. Langara went away fully convinc'd that He had met with the utmost politeness He Ever could have wish'd for and much more than He could have expected. He Seemed a good sort of man; was Very highly displeased with the French. This Day Several Vessels came In, some from Cork and from other places; also one was brought In Loaded with Barley, intended for Cadiz. We have not as yet had any Live Stock from Barbary; nor do I hear of any Mode Settled about getting any! Several Town Market Boats are over there, and the *Apollo* Frigate went over to Barbary this Evening.

Sund 13. Easterly wind. The Signal made for Sailing. The Colonel went on Board both Admirals with planns &c, &c, and took Leave of the Prince. A most fortunate Event took place this Morning, viz., the Men of War that went up to Minorca with the Convoy (this Day fortnight) return'd Just as our Fleet was getting under sail! Nothing could have happened more favorably. The chief part of the Fleet got out this Evening with a very fine Wind. Great hurry just now all over the Garrison. All those that could were getting off as fast as possible. All the Family of the Powndes going &c &c.

Mond 14. Easterly wind. The whole Fleet left Gibraltar this Day. It will not be amiss if I make a few remarks on some fortunate events that has attended this Fleet from the Day they left England, which was upon Christmass Day 1779. Some Days after they left Portsmouth it was not known whether the whole or a part was coming to this place. However after they had obey'd the Signal from Sir G. Rodney and had received his orders they proceeded on their passage here. They fell In with the Valuable Fleet of Carraco Ships, took them to the amount of £400,000! Then they met with part of the Spainish Fleet, took 7 of their Line of Battle. The rest of that Fleet under command of Don Luis de Cordova had gone only Six Days before into Cadiz, not suspecting any such Fleet as ours, which indeed shews how greatly the Spainish Court had been deceived by the French; for it is very certain had they keep a look out it must have been known. Our Fleet had the Satisfaction to get all the Convoy for this Garrison Safe; and relieved us to the utmost of our wishes; from thence sent off to Minorca all that Garrison stood in Need of, viz., Money and cloathing for Troops. The Wind carried all that Convoy up, and was so much favor'd in returning that it was only barely possible to form such a wish with any degree of success! Not only that, but what made it still more fortunate, they came back upon the very Day the Admiral was getting out of this Harbour; it was indeed the very thing We all most wished for, tho' hardly

34

could have expected. They sailed with a fine Wind, which lasted as 14th February 1780. long as to carry Them where they wished, and by the Information of a Vessel from the West who came In upon the 20th We learn that the Fleet was met with in so favorable a Latitude that it gives all manner of prospect of a quick passage home, If so it may not be at all impossible for the whole of these Circumstances to have happened in the course of Ten Weeks ! to Say Nothing of what may fall out in their passage home, or indeed of other matters which I have not taken notice of in form, all adding to the peculiar favor of Providence,—and Surely never was a more Remarkable Period in History; of a Succesful Passage and a fortunate Supply to a Blockaded Garrison.

We now hear by the arrival of some English officers and other Prisoners belonging to our Fleet who are sent In from Cadiz that when the Spainiards which were in Brest Harbour heard of our Grand Fleet and of our having taken Don Juan Langara, they directly left Brest and with 20 Sail of Line sailed for Gibraltar, in hopes to meet our Fleet or to Force this Harbour. A Violent Storm attacked them and has in a great degree drove them to destructiom ; they are getting as fast as they can into Cadiz, but for the most part Unfitt for service, Those that are not as yet arrived may very likely meet with our Fleet home. If they do they will Stand a bad chance. The report now is that the Spainiards are so totaly displeased with their French Friends and so provoked at what has happened to themselves that it is pretty Certain they mean to Try all their Efforts to gain this place, for they have repeatedly told our English officers, they only want and wish for Gibraltar ! " Give up that to us, they say, and all will be Well."

From the 14th of Feb, the Day on which our Fleet left us, Nothing very particular Happened till the 25th, except the whole attention of the Garrison to get into safe places all the Stores and provisions. The Boom which Barcelo made over at Algezira has been taken up ever since our Admiral and Fleet Left Gibraltar. They have hang'd Several Soldiers in their Camp, but that has not hindered more of their Wolona Guards to come to Us.

Fry 25. Westerly wind. A Vessel arrived from Farro, Loaded with Wine &c for this place, but the most Valuable part was a Number of Letters of different dates to many persons in the Garrison I had the Satisfaction of Receiving one letter of 12th Nov from Mrs Green, and one of same date from Mrs Nicolls and one of 12th Dec from her. It afforded great Satisfaction. We had a large Company at Dinner, Genl and Ladies, the Davies, Gledstanes &c. The Weather fair but cold. Barcelo seems busy. A Vessel arrived to Day with wine and other articles frome Minorca. The Small Pox is beginning to be very fatal to the Children. All Means are tried to obtain Leave to Innoculate but as yet to no purpose.

26th February,
1780.

Saturd 26. Easterly wind. We all begin to get letters wrote in hopes the Store Ships will be soon going. I try all Means to get Charlotte inoculated but cannot obtain leave.

Sund 27. Easterly wind, very fine morning, and continued so all Day. I did not stir out being not well. 3 Line of Battle Ships and other Ships are gone over to Barcelo this morning. A Neapolitan Ship came into the Bay, was brought to by a Gun from Kings Bastion, She sent off a Boat and said she was last from Minorca, Loaded with Oil and Honey, bound to London. She anchored near the Old Mole ; and afterwards sent off a Boat to Fort St Philip. This should make Us doubt if she is a Friend. However in the Night she went from her Station, and was seen at Algezira the next Morning !

Mond 28. Easterly wind. Colonel engaged all forenoon at Col Ross, and the rest of the Colonels, relating to the Circumstances of the Rank between Lt Col Trigg, Lt Col Craig and Lt Col Mackenzie. N.B. It is to be referred to the Commander in Chief in England.

Tuesd 29. Easterly wind, very fine Day. Nothing very particular all this Day. Several People in Evening. A great many Northern Lights in air. No News of the Prisoners that were expected. Yesterday the Troops had for the first time Salt Fish delivered to them instead of Meat and some Rice and Peas, not any Butter ; which occasioned great discontent ; as it seems hard to oblige them to take the fish in place of Meat and not to give them a little Butter with it. We hear it is to be changed. N.B. This Evening they all Received a Small Allowance of Butter, but they are dissatisfied.

March 1st. *Wed*y. Westerly Wind, and very fine Day. It was in Orders this Day that Capt Lt Witham of the Royal Artillery is to be Aid de Camp in the room of Capt Patterson of the Same Corps.

Thurs 2. Westerly wind, fine Day. This Morning 2 Sailors came over from Barcelo's Fleet in a little Boat. They belong'd to this place, and were taken some Weeks agoe from out of a Towns Vessel which Used to cruize about. They have been kept on board one of the Spainish Men of War. They bring Word that there is 3 Battalions of the Spainish Troops gone from the Camp, which indeed we have known, by finding Many of their Tents struck. It is also said They are gone to Strengthen some part belonging to the Spainiards.

Fry 3rd. Westerly wind, fine soft Day. We had a large Company at dinner and more in Evening,—Gen Boyd, Phipps, &c, and Fancourt in evening,—all very well. No change in any publick Business.

Saturd 4th. Easterly wind. A good deal of wind. The Col: Rode out, The Day continued fine. Find I have got a great cold and some other complaints. Mr Holloway dined at the Convent. We were quite alone in Evening.

Sun 5. Easterly wind and a Dull looking Morning. At Noon it blew exceedingly hard and continued so for more than an hour. At

last it began to Rain which abatted the wind. N.B. The New ^{5th March, 1780.}
Moon was about this time. We had a good many Gentlemen at
Supper. The Small Pox raging very much and very fatal.

Mond 6. Easterly wind. Hear that an Inhabitant, Mr Brooks, is
going away this Night on board a Swedish Vessel. I send one letter
to Mrs Green and one to Mrs Nicolls. Not very well this evening
and out of Spirits.

Tuesd 7. Easterly wind. The Ship did not go last Night. The
Col: writes this Day to Mrs Boddington and to Fisher, also to Genl
Skinner. Genl Boyd sent us a hind Qr of Wild Boar. The Col and
Mr Holloway Sup't out at Capt Loyd. Our letters went under care
of Mr Brooks who went on board this even.

Wed 8. Easterly wind. Find the Ship is gone last Night. This
Day we find that the Enemy are sending away Many Articles from
the Camp, and loading Vessels at the Orange Grove. Likewise it was
observed that the officers Baggage was taken away as fast as they
could send: Trunks and all Sorts of Camp Equipage. We had a very
large Party in the Evening, Mrs Booth and Family, &c, &c, 16 in
all.

Thurs 9. Easterly wind, fine Day. Nothing more than a Parley
from the Enemy today. Went out to Capt Phipps at dinner; the Col
Rode out all forenoon. Hear that Commander Elliott had sent out to
the Enemy to know why those English Prisoners were not sent In, and
to request the Don J. Langara would be return'd into Gibraltar, unless
we had our own People sent.

Fry 10. Easterly wind, fine Day. Dull and Cold. The Col
walked out. At Home in the evening, quite alone. A Parley from
the Enemy this Day.

Saturd 11. Easterly wind, fine at first but turned Dull and Cold
in forenoon. The Colonel dined at Convent. At home in evening,
only ourselves. A Parley from the Enemy to Day.

Sund 12. Easterly wind; fine in the forenoon, but Dull and Cold
at Night. I walked out before Dinner and called upon Several
Persons. Hear that the English Prisoners are coming In from
Spain. There are two Flaggs of Truce gone from Us, and three Row
Galleys are coming from the Orange Grove to Us. The Windmill is
moving from where Capt Evelegh first fix'd it. It is to go to
Windmill Hill.

Mond 13. Easterly wind, fine clear Morning. The Prisoners
came last Night and are going on board the Men of War this Day.
3 men of the 72nd Regt Deserted from off the Hill last Night, and
one of the same Regt went off 2 Days agoe. This Day the Provisions
were first delivered out by the Month to each officer. Each Man's
Share is as follows; I mean each officer's Ration. I shall set down
by Way of Mem^m the Order that was given on this subject. N.B.
There is some small difference between the officers and the private

13th March, 1780.

men's Provisions. N.B. Upon the whole this order has not given satisfaction. The Fish, tho' very good is objected to ; at least the being obliged to receive it for so long a time, particularly as it is supposed there is such a quaintity of Provisions in Store. This evening 2 of the Deserters of the 72nd taken, the other not known.

Plan for Victualing the Garrison for one Month ; to Commence on Monday the 13th March. Officers of the Army and Civil department, to draw for a Month's Provisions at one time, and in one order. (Bread excepted, which will be Issued weekly) and if they leave any in the office it must be entire Rations, which will be accounted for every three Months.

It is conjectured this will be thought Disagreable, for as yet no Method has been found which Way those Provisions are to be paid for which may now Remain due to Individuals in the office. The whole of this department is now in the Hands of the Q.M. Genl.— New Lords, New Laws, the Agent Victu^{or} has nothing now to Do !

One Month's Single Ration for an Officer.—Beef 3 lbs ; Pork 2 lbs ; Fish 9 lbs ; Pease 8 pints ; Wheat 5 lbs ; Rice 4 lbs ; Oatmeal 6 pints ; Butter 40 oz.

N.B. Colonel Green has Ten Rations.

One Month's Ration for a Soldier.—First and third week as follows :—Pork 1 lb ; Fish 2½ lbs ; Pease 2 pints ; Rice 1 lb ; Oatmeal 1½ lbs ; Butter 5 oz ; Wheat ½ lb ; Raisons ¼ lb.

Second and fourth week as follows :—Beef 1½ lbs ; Fish 2 lbs ; Rice 1 lb ; Wheat 1½ lbs ; Oatmeal 1½ pints ; Raisons ¼ lb ; Butter 5 oz.

Each Hospital Per Week as follows :—Beef 2 lbs ; Fish 2 lbs ; Rice 1 lb ; Flour 1 lb ; Oatmeal 3 pints ; Raisons 1½ lbs ; Butter 5 oz.

N.B. All the above took place Mond 13th March 1780.

Tues 14. Easterly wind. Dull Morning. I went out to the Mount in the Post chaise for the first time,—took Charlotte. The Day did not turn out quite so fine as I wished. Hear there was a man of La Motte's deserted from Forbes last night. The Town Boat, call'd the *Fly*, came over from Barbary, brings a few Fowls and Eggs, also a packet of letters, none for Us—says there is an English Vessel now at Tangier from Eng^{d,} in 15 days from Portsmouth. In the afternoon there was firing from Europa at a Xebeque that was trying to Attack a Brig that was bringing In a small Prize. She proves to be an English privatter, call'd the *Maidstone*. She was In here and went away about three weeks agoe. Has brought In a little Boat and got safe to the New Mole. The *Enterprize* fired at the Xebeque but did not reach Her. It is this Day reported that there is a large Army of French intended to come into the Spainish Camp to attack this Garrison, and that they are Daily expected.

Wed 15. Easterly wind, a very Dull Morning. It rained very 15th March, early. Find myself exceedingly indisposed, could not get up to 1780. Breakfast. This Day a Court Martial sitting upon the two Deserters of 72nd: Colonel Picton 12th Regt, President, 4 Field officers, 8 Captains. In the afternoon a Cutter came from the West; she came from Scilly, had fallen In with a Spainish Frigate of 36 Guns off Cadiz and had Received Some damage. N.B. The beginning of this Month Mr Raleigh Secy to the Gov[r] was appointed Commissary for the Exchange of Prisoners. The hurry and Daily hopes and Expectations which now prevailed, particularly in Weak Minds, began to Affect me, and I grew exceedingly ill. My Head and Eyes very bad, hardly indeed am able to write this, and fear I am going to be very ill. It was the same with me some weeks ago, but as I only write for the Amusement of myself and if ever it so happen for my own family's Information in a few points,—so I am the less anxious about the Stile or Manner. No one in evening.

Thursd 16. Easterly wind, tolerable Day. Find myself rather better but not in spirits. Nothing new this Day. Very little to be got in the Market this Day. The child and two of the Maids went to the Mt in afternoon. Fine Night. A Cutter came In from the West, call'd the *Alert*. She was bringing In a prize. She is a fine Privateer. She lost the prize. It was taken into Algezira.

Fry 17. Easterly wind, very fine Morning and continued so all day. Hear that the two Deserters were to be shott, the time not yet fix'd. Several Signals up at our Look out; from the East; and in the afternoon a Large Number of Vessels going through, supposed to be a Dutch Convoy. Find myself very much indisposed this Day with a Severe Cold; which has affected me for above a Month past.

Saturd 18*th*. Easterly wind, fine Day. Capt Loyd upon Batterys to Day. Fired in the Evening. I was not Well this Day or in Spirits, find the Smallest Vexation hurts my Health, and I feel pains in Consequence of it.

Sund 19. Easterly wind, fine Day. In the afternoon the Enemy fired a Feu-de-Joye in their Camp, as did likewise all the Men of War over at Algezira. The whole Line turned out and appeared a large Body. Various opinions formed. Both yesterday and to Day we fired more shott than for some Weeks past. The Gov[r] has also given orders to the captains upon the Batterys to fire at the Patroles in the Night. Capt Shands upon the Batterys to Day. One of the two soldiers lately Try'd is Reprieved this afternoon. The other is to be Shot Tomorrow.

Mond 20. Easterly wind, a very fine Warm Morning. Hear that the Rejoicing in the Camp was on occasion of a Son Born to the Prince of Asturias, Son to the King of Spain. One of their officers told one of ours, when they met on a Parley that such an event was hourly expected and wish'd for. This is the first Son. We find by

20th March, 1780.

the appearance of their Men Under Arms that there is still a large Number of Troops in the Camp, and also a Battalion over at Algezira. Notwithstanding it has been said They had sent away a great many Regts. This forenoon the Man of 72nd was shott. He had formerly belong'd to 58th and had married the Daughter of the Sergeant Major of that Regt who was sent for to the Govr of this Garrison some years agoe by Sir Willm How who had a great regard for the Sergeant Major. He made him an officer and he is now a Capt in a Regt in America. This Soldier's Wife is in England. His Name is Traverss. He seem'd to feel for his Wife and Her Father.

Tuesd 21. Easterly Wind, pleasant Day. We Kill'd a Small Cow this forenoon for the Use of the Family, and sent away as presents the following Pieces. The Cow weighed 400 lbs. A Sir Loin to General Boyd; a part of the Ribs to Colonel Godwin; a piece of the Loin to Roast and a small piece to Boil for Capt Phipps; a part of the forequarter and a little piece for Soup for Colonel Gledstanes; a part of the Sir Loin to Doctor Baynes; a part of the Ribs for the Engineer Mess; a piece for Boiling for Mrs Skinner; a piece for Roasting for Mrs Booth; a piece for Roasting, Capt Evelegh; a Round for Mrs Power; and a Shin or two for some Sick families; the Head and Liver between Serjeant Grant and one of our Married Servants. N.B. We had been offer'd 25 Guineas for it and I daresay might have had £30, for Every Body was Selling as Dear as they thought proper, but I detested the imposing practice. This Cow Turn'd out exceeding Good Meat and was very Acceptable at this Juncture. It was the 2nd of my Cows. I have now 2 Cows and a young Heifer left. This is the first Field Day this season. The Colonel went out at Landport this afternoon. He saw the Captain of Landport Guard, as he was Walking out, near the Meadow, with two Gentlemen that are Here on their way to Algiers, one of them Brother to Mr Wilks. The Col thought it wrong to go so far with strangers, particularly leaving the Guard. The Captn ought always to be at his Post.

Wed 22. Easterly wind, a Dull looking Morning. The Captain that was at Landport yesterday was put Under arrest this morning at Gun Fire; by order from the Govr for leaving his Guard yesterday and going as far as the Devil's Tower with those two Gentlemen. It is Captn Duff of 58th.

Thursd 23. Easterly wind; a Dull Day. Had Company to Dine. I write a long letter to My Sister and sent it by the Sloop Privateer, the *Alert*. Find myself much indisposed.

Fry 24. Easterly wind. Dull Day. The Sloop sailed last Night. 2 Line of Battle Ships and 1 Frigate gone from Algezira. Capt Duff out of Arrest, no consequences having follow'd, except a Caution given to all captains at Landport Guard for the Future.

(To be continued).

A LADY'S EXPERIENCES IN THE GREAT SIEGE OF GIBRALTAR (1779-83).

BEING THE DIARY FROM 1ST JUNE, 1779, TO 13TH JUNE, 1781, OF MRS. GREEN, THE WIFE OF LIEUT.-COLONEL GREEN, CHIEF ENGINEER OF GIBRALTAR (AFTERWARDS LIEUT.-GENERAL SIR WILLIAM GREEN, BART., CHIEF ENGINEER OF GREAT BRITAIN, 1786—1802).

(Continued).

Saturd 25.   Easterly wind, a fine Day.   Find myself but very indifferent, am very much out of Spirits on many accounts, as I meet with many Vexations which I did not expect.

Sund 26. Easter Day.   Easterly wind.   A very fine Warm Morning.   I walked out before Dinner with the Child, find myself very indifferent whilst out and come home very Low.   A Man of the 39th and one of 73rd Deserted last Night from the Back of the Hill. We were quite alone in the Evening.   I went to See Mrs Lewis this Day.   The Small Pox in many parts of the Garrison.   No Innoculation allowed of as yet.

Mond 27.   Easterly wind, very Dull indifferent Day.   The Colonel exceedingly displeased with publick Business, and still more after Breakfast continued greatly displeased all Day.   He went to the American Club.   N.B. This is the first Meeting of the American Club.*   He is President.   Came home at 9 in the evening in tolerable spirits.   It began to Rain in the evening.   Children Dieing every Day. George taken very ill in the Evening ; pain in foot.

Tuesd 28.   Easterly wind.   It Blow'd and rain'd exceedingly all Night, and so bad a Morning that the Review of the 12th was obliged to be put off.   It continued a very Wet Day.   Hear that Colonel Mawhood has broke his Arm by a fall as He was going to the Southward last Night.   The Same discontent in the Colonel and the same Causes.   N.B. This Circumstance first began by an affair of Lt Skinner's, relating to Some few Libertys taken concerning the Cattle.   N.B. Capt Evelegh has got a piece of Ground allotted to him, the same where The Wind Mill was first put up, which was begun and fail'd ; all Under the Direction of Capt Evelegh.

Wed 29.   Easterly wind.   The Morning pretty fine.   Hardenburgh's Regt Reviewed.   The Day continues good.   A visit from Col Ross.   George still ill in his room.

* See Sept. 14, 1780.

Thursd 30.   Easterly wind ; a fine Morning.   The 52nd reviewed The Govr has given the name of Mill Mount to the piece of Groun which he has given Capt Evelegh.   N.B. It is where that Gentlema had Erected the Windmill, and without any Success.   Several Ladie at the Review.

Fry 31.   Easterly in Morning ; turn'd out a very fine Day.   The 39tl reviewed, and to the Astonishment of every Body Col Ross attende as Lt Col to the Regt.   He had never been with them at any o their Field Days, or done any Duty, for Many Months.   It was no known to any of the officers that He would be there ; but just befor the Regt went on He sent to Col Kellet and inform'd him He ha let the Govr know He intended to fall in with the Regt.   In th same time Genl Boyd* went on to the Parade but never Joyn'd th Regt, only as a Spectator as on other Days.   The whole went o pretty well ; better indeed than it could be expected, as it wa very Reasonable to think the men were taken at a disadvantage b the changing the Commanding officer that very Morning.   There wa no Regimental Breakfast, every body went as they chose.   The whol Regt dined as others have done at the Gov^rs.   Genl Boyd also dine there in his General's Uniform with his Aid de Camps, not makin himself Colonel of the 39th the whole Day.   All pass'd very well, bu he or Col Ross did not speak to each other.   Many People thinl these two Gentleman will never Settle the Coolness that is betwee them ; as the Dislike seems to increase.   They are both ver Valuable Characters.   In the Evening Colonel Ross came here. was alone at the first ; and as Usual heard all the Story.   All Ende Well.

During the course of this last Month the Enemy may have bee rather Slow in their business of all kinds.   Towards the last fe Days they seem beginning to show more Spirits.   Certainly they ar not going away.   Would to God They either would leave us or sho themselves in Earnest.   We cannot be said to enjoy any great degre of Ease or Comfort just now.   The kind of Necessity that the Gov has found out to change the Provisions has occasioned a great deal c discontent.   The Troops never objected to any Method when a appearance was of a Serious Nature, but now they seem to think i hard to be obliged to eat so much Salt Fish when it is Well know there is an amazing Quaintity of Beef and Pork !   Salt Fish withou the proper Sauces is but poor Diet, and particularly in the Hot Season now coming on.

Saturd April 1st.   Westerly Wind.   This Morning was very fine A Hanoverian Regt, Redan's, was Reviewed.   All very Well.   / Deserter came In from Spain, the Wolona Guards.   Colonel and M

* General Boyd was Colonel, and Colonel Ross, Lieut.-Colonel of th 39th.

Holloway dined with Lt Cuppage. George still Confined to his
Room. Gun Fir'd at 9 oclock this Evening.

Sund 2. Westerly wind, a fine looking Morning. Set down to
write letters to England in hopes the Store Ships will sail soon. The
Guards Mount at 7 in the Morning. N.B. Every Sunday there is
the Same kind of publick Works going on as on Week Days, and a
Continuation of many Unpleasant Circumstances. This Morning the
Enemy Seem to have large Quaintities of Straw and other Stores
landing at the Usual Places ; by which it does not appear as if they
had any Idea of leaving the Camp. We now most heartily wish they
would show their real Intentions.

Mond 3. Westerly wind. The *Porcupine* Frigate sail'd last Night
for Minorca and Algiers, on board of which was Mr Wilks &c, and
Mr Davisson. Genl Boyd sent Us a very fine hind Quarter of
English Mutton yesterday. George still very ill and confin'd to his
room since this Day Week. Doctor Baynes informs me that the
Small Pox broke out upon a Man of the Highland Regt on Fryday
last. N.B. This is the first Soldier that has got that Disorder. At
this time there is a Number of Children ill with it. Captain Knowles
a Master of a Transport Well known in Gibraltar, and who has been
here a long time, Died rather Suddenly. It Rain'd this Evening. It
is now Supposed the Gov will allow of Innoculation, as He has said
He would have no objection to it whenever the Troops took the
Small Pox.

Tuesd 4. Westerly wind. A Review of the 56th Regt. A fine
Morning. Charlotte was greatly indisposed all Night quite Burning
with Heat. I gave her one of the Small Pills, and she Grew very ill
afterwards. Doctor Baynes is of the opinion she is Breeding the
Small Pox. The child has not been quite Well these last Ten Days.
She continued greatly indisposed all this Day and was Bath'd in
Warm Water going to Bed.

Wed 5. Westerly wind. De la Motts Regt Reviewed. This
Morning the *Fly* Pacquet Boat came In from Barbary, brings a few
Fowls, oranges, and onions,— all Selling exceedingly Dear. Fowls 2
Dollars a piece, oranges half a Rial, onions 2 Rials pr pound. Brings
Word that the Brig belonging to Mr Mowbarry and Mackellar was
drove into Tetuan Bay two Nights agoe by contrary winds as she
was coming over and is now safe there. Charlotte much better in
Evening and the fever most over. George exceeding ill.

Thursd 6. Westerly wind. This morning 2 Market Boats came
In from Barbary, bring a happy supply of Bullocks, 36, and Some
Fowls, Oranges, &c, all Selling very Dear, Fowls 2 Dollars, and
upon the whole full as dear as that which came yesterday, says that
the Brig is still in Tetuan Bay. They bring good News of some
Engagement which was confirm'd by a Servant who came from the
Consul (Mr Logie) to our Gov to inform him that our Fleet had an

<table>
<tr><td>6th April,
1780.</td><td>

Engagement with the Spainiards going home from hence.   Charlott had a very good Night and continues quite well to Day. Georg exceedingly ill and in Violent pain, not able to Move in his Bed witl out help. A Deserter came In this Morning of the Wolona Guard: The Soldier of the Highland Regt is well and has had an exceedingl fine Sort of Small Pox. No Innoculation allowed of as yet. Mos People are displeased at this as it is certainly much better for th men and poor children to have this Disorder now than when it i Warmer.   For my own part I am exceedingly Anxious for our Dea little Girl; and did it depend wholly upon myself I would not as any leave.

</td></tr>
</table>

Fry 7.   Westerly wind.   The 58th Review.   Hear a furthe account of the Engagement between our Fleet and the French goin from hence to Eng^d.   Also We hear that Sir George Rodney was a Madeira upon the 19th of Feb^ry.   He sailed from hence upon th 14th.   The Colonel dined at Genl Boyd's this Day.   Mr Hollowa with me.   George continues exceedingly ill.   Charlotte quite wel The *Fly* Pacquet Boat went to Barbary this Evening.   The Fowl 20 Rials a piece.

Saturd 8.   Westerly wind.   The 72nd Review.   Bought som Veal for which I gave 6 Rials per lb.   Resolve to go to the Mount a the Weather was so fine.   George still Confined to his Room.   Go a New Hat and Silver Band &c for the Postilion.   We have no bought any of the Fowls.   The Col: not exceeding well pleased at th Mode of carrying on Business.   N.B. Nor is any of the Command ing officers satisfied,—so little attention shew'd to Them.

Sund 9.   Westerly wind, fine Morning.   Went to the Mount in th chaise to Breakfast, took Charlotte and her Maid staid there ti Tuesday Evening.   On Monday a Boat arrived from Barbary, bring Word of a Certainty of our having had an Engagement with th French, and also that an English Fleet was hourly expected a Cadiz.

Mon 10.   Cold Westerly wind.   George rather better.

Tuesd 11.   Westerly wind.   Nothing particular.   Small Pox rag ing very bad, children dying every Day.   Din'd at the Mount an came Home in Evening on account of some Business.   Find I hav a Cold in my Head.   Commodore at the Mount.

Wed 12.   Westerly wind but rather Cool.   Great Uneasines about some *Engineering* Business, the Colonel much hurt at it an had some *particular conversations* with Capt Phipps and Cap Evelegh &c.   The Small Pox increases.   I am very much indispose in the afternoon.   This evening about a Quarter after 8 we were a Surprised by the Alarm Drums Beating.   We had several Gentleme in the Parlour, who all Run out, but soon returned bringing Word i was nothing of any Consequence, only a Fire amongst some Shaving of Wood in an out House belonging to the Convent, Supposed t

have been set on Fire by a Squibb from Some Children at play. 12th Ap
This Night about 11 oclock Capt Leslie of the *Enterprize* fired 4 or 1780.
5 Guns, not known at what !

Thursd 13. Westerly Wind. This Morning at Gun Fire two Market
Boats, or rather one, the other being the Privateer, *Saucy Jack*,
arrived from Tangier with a Packet of Letters and some Bullocks,
Fowls, and Oranges &c. We Rec^d some letters and 4 News Papers.
I had one letter from My Daughter Nicolls, dated Jan 28th by which
We learn that our Son's Commission of Captain was dated 24th Decr
1779. Our oldest paper dated 15th Jan. the latest Feb 5th. All
well in our Family at that time. The Colonel also Rec^d his acct
from his Agents. I have had a very bad N^t and am Lame, exceedingly ill so as to keep my Bed, fear I shall grow worse as the
Complaint seems to increase in all Limbs.

Fryd 14. Westerly wind. A Deserter came In, brings a confused
account of the Enemy's Intention to Advance. I went down to
dinner but found a very great pain in my Left Knee. Quite alone in
evening. Several Guns were Fired in the Bay at 10 oclock at Night.

Saturd 15. Westerly wind. Find myself growing exceeding bad ;
a most Violent Headache ; likewise my Leg and Knee, could not get
up. Hear that the Firing was occasioned by the Arrival of the *Hyena*
Frigate from Eng^d 20 days from Portsmouth. Capt Thomson has
brought very Particular Dispatches for the Govr and Commodore
Elliot. We hear she is likely to go back very soon ; must therefore
try to send home some letters if it is in my power to write ; but I
now keep my Bed, not being able to bear the Moving. I sit up and
wrote a long letter to my sister this Morning and inclosed one I had
wrote in part since the first of this Month to my Mother. This was
all I could do to Day. I Rec^d a letter by this Frigate from Lady Rich
from Portsmouth ; fear it will not be in my power to Answer it as I
am exceedingly ill.

Sund 16. Easterly wind. The Frigate seems likely to be going.
Every Body is hurrying to write letters. The Colonel Busy in getting
Public papers ready. I sit up in bed and write a long letter to my
Son on his Promotion. This Day my pains moved into my Right
Leg and nothing can exceed the Agonies I am In. An other Deserter
came In, brings In a further Confirmation of the Enemy's Intention ;
in bed all Day.

Mond 17. Westerly wind. Ships not gone. Am worse this Day than
yesterday, and at Night beyond all possibility of bearing it with any
Degree of Patience. The Small Pox Raging greatly and has got
among all the Regts. A Man of the Soldier Artificers exceedingly
bad with it. No Innoculation yet !

Tuesd 18. Westerly wind. Have had the Worst Night I ever
experienced in my Life. Write this in my Bed. Continue exceedingly bad at Day and at Night.

Wed 19. Easterly wind. Not able to get up. Take Dove Powders. Ships not gone. The Garrison very Low and Dull.

Thursd 20. Easterly wind. The same. The *Edgar* Commodo Elliot and the *Hyena* Frigate Capt Thomson sailed, and in the afte noon Admiral Barcelo went out.

Fry 21. Easterly wind. *Colonel and Gov'* upon the Parade. Fi myself a very little Easier. Take more of James Powders; can r sit up yet. The Man of the Highland Regt Recover'd.

Saturd 22. Westerly wind. Seem a little Easier; set up a part the Day. The Man of the Artificer Company very bad.

Sund 23. Westerly wind. I was taken up in the Course of t Day but not able to Stand. 7 Men Died of the Highland Re between last Night and this Evening, of a Flux and Fever. Th had lost near 100 before. Barcelo return'd to Algezira. T Even about 8 oclock a very bright and Remarkable Meteor w seen in the Sky, resembling a burning, flying Kite,—Viz., a Blazi Star; Seem to take its direction towards the Queen of Spai Chair. Find myself tolerably Easy when going to Bed. My Fc greatly swelled.

Mond 24. Westerly wind. Had a much better Night than I ha of late, tho' did not Sleep but very little after 3 oclock. Got up at but only could be set in a Chair by the Bed Side. Rather low Day. Barcelo has return'd back to his Station two Days. The Sm Pox exceedingly raging; Children also Dieing. Hawkins of t company very bad with it.

Tuesd 25. Westerly wind. My Lameness no better; but hac little Rest last Night,—not a bit better able to Move. Set all D in my Chair, between Window and Bed. Charlotte got a bad Cou; Mackellar's Vessel arrived on Sunday from Barbary.

Wed 26. Westerly wind. Did not Sleep quite so Well but fi my Leg rather Easier when I got up. If I continue so to Morrc mean to be taken into Dressing Room. This Even Hawkins di Col: and Mr Holloway dined at Genl Boyd's, Supt at Phipps. T Day a Spainish line of Battle Ship anchor'd near Point Negro. S remained all Day and Evening.

Thursd 27. Easterly wind. A Boat arrived from Malaga, l from Tangier, with oranges, Eggs, and oil. She is going to Far This forenoon Don Barcelo and two Line of Battle Ships got Un Sail and went towards the West. I came out this Day to my Dre ing Room, being brought out by two Women, after having been my Bed Room 14 days, Wrote some more in a letter to r Daughter Nicolls in hopes to get an opportunity to send it. N.B did not mention that the Troops had Soft Bread issued out to th upon the 24th for the first time since the Fleet left us, (they hav had Biscuit all that Period). Great complaints now making abr Salt Fish.

Fry 28.   Westerly wind.   Hear that Barcelo was return'd, and also that all thoughts of the Store Ships going was over, it being impossible to let them have any Convoy.   A Boat arrived from Malaga yesterday that is to go to Portugal as soon as possible.   Very Lame still. 28th Apr 1780.

Salurd 29.   Westerly wind.   Obliged to be brought out the Same as before.   Much confused talk of the Enemy's Intention to Fire upon the 1st of May.   They are landing Stores of all Sorts at Point Negro.   This Day and for these Days past the Colonel has been rather Low and Dull, owing to many Unpleasant Circumstances in business.

Sund 30.   Westerly wind.   Brought out again by the two Women. N.B. I try'd all I could in the Course of Yesterday to assist myself and Strove all that my Strength would allow to Stand, but it was attended by my growing a great deal Worse for it.   The Same Unpleasant talk of to Morrow Firing.   This Evening about half past 9 a Sudden Fire broke out in the Enemy's Camp.   We did not at first know what to make of it.   It continued to burn very Smartly indeed for half an hour.   It appeared as if it was behind the Camp. We heard their Drums beating most of the time.   N.B. Upon the 16th of this month the following Memorandum was given to the several Adj^{ts} at Orderly time, but it was not put down as Orders. I was then so ill that I omitted to set it down in its proper place.

· "The Governor permits all officers who have enclosed and Cultivated ground to keep it during their residence in the Garrison on Condition that they shall send to the publick Market all the produce they do not make use of themselves and that they do plant Trees."

Various opinions form'd in Consequence of the above; to think what could induce the Govr to give out such Recomendations, particularly as he has encouraged Several officers of late to enclose Grounds &c, and also giving so large a place upon the Mountain to Capt Evelegh, and also at the South to Capt Witham.   However it cannot affect Us at the Mount; ours being upon a different footing, as the Colonel pays a Yearly Ground Rent into the Revenue, and We do not allow ourselves to think the Govr has anything to do with our property.   Mount Pleasant has now been near 5 years improvement and may most likely turn out of the Utmost advantage to the Garrison.

Thus ended the Month of April, and it is not very Easy to tell how exceedingly Uncomfortable all Ranks of People now are.   This Circumstance of the Generals Refusing to allow of Innoculation has hurt all degrees of People.   Several Men are quite Miserable at not being allow'd to Innoculate—12 men in one Regt were anxious—and it is the More to be Wonder'd at as the Govr did actually say He would not have any objections if it once got amongst the Troops, which it has now; and likewise has been already fatal.

Mond May 1st. Westerly wind, not so bright a Morning as (late. All has remained perfectly quiet from the Enemy, so that ver little is to be depended upon from what is mentioned by flyin Reports. We can plainly See where the Fire was last Night. It : in the Rear of the Camp amongst some Hutts, most likely Sutler Hutts, and little shops. There seems to have been a good Man Burnt, indeed it was a very considerable time Burning, and We knov they could have no Supply of Water. This Day keeps very Dull an Hott, looking like Rain. Various Reports still with Respect to th Enemy's Intentions, and the Inhabitants, Idly giving Way to thei fears are all flying out to the South. This was the Second Monthl: Meeting of the American Club. The Colonel was not very Well however He went and Return'd in the Evening perfectly cool, an better than when He went out. About 7 it began to Rain an continued a fine Shower till 10, when I write this. My Lamenes still very Troublesome, not being able to stand. A General Cour Martial this Day upon a Man of 39th for theft, Col Cockra President.

Tuesd 2. Westerly wind, a pleasant Morning. Here the Enem are busy landing Mortars and all sorts of Stores at Point Negrc Find myself very little better as to my Lameness; and am ver Low spirited most of this Day. Mrs Phipps &c call'd. Col: prett well. This Morning Doctor Baynes tells me He has been with th Govr and had talked with him about the Small Pox, and asked hir this one Question; If it happened in a family where there were Mor than one child, would it not be a better Way to Innoculate the Res of that family? as it was not to be doubted They would get it, an it would be the means of its being Sooner over. He answered: No by no means! He could not answer it to his Conscience. What th Gov^{rs} Meaning is I know not; but I do think He ought to make point of getting this cruel Disorder as soon over as possible we knowing the Violent Season coming on; and also to comfort man anxious Parents and others.

Wed 3. Westerly wind. Am still Lame. The Colonel not ver Well and did not go to Parade. Many Idle Reports about th Enemys advancing and it was actually said They had begun to throv up Ground on this Side the Lines; and that two Engineers wer seen in the Round Tower, as it is call'd, upon the Neutral Grounc It was afterwards Well known it was two Dogs that had bee hunting about and had torn up the Ground. I saw the very office who first observed them and absolutely distinguish'd the Differen Colours of those very Dogs,—the officer at Forbes Guard,—He call'(up to the officer at the Lines and told him what it really was; but h was displeased and ask'd if He was not a Judge between 2 Dogs an 2 Men, upon which He (the officer at the Lines) made his report t the Govr who sent Word to the Capt of the Batterys that if H

48

observed any Troops, or even Partys to assemble on this Side their 3rd May, Lines, that He should fire all the Guns that He could bring to bear 1780. that Way. However all Remained perfectly quiet.

Thursd 4. Easterly wind early this Morning. I finished a letter to My Sister and sent that and an other to my Daughter Nicolls which I finished Yesterday (tho' I had begun it to her upon the 20th of April) and inclosed them to Lt Amphlett of 39th as it is expected He will go in a Boat to Farro this Evening. The Col: had a Walk to Rosia this forenoon, did not come home till near three, which according to Custom Tired him, and he was very much out of *Sorts* in the afternoon.

Mem^{m.} It was an Unpleasant afternoon. My Leg has been in a good deal of pain all Day. N.B. Every Day there are children Dieing with the Small Pox and also a very bad Fever. The Man of the 39th is to be Executed on Monday. The Col: very much *disturb'd* in Even. My Leg grew Violently bad at Night, obliged to be carried by all three Women to Bed.

Fry 5. Easterly wind. Lt Amphlett went last Night. Find myself very indifferent indeed, but for many reasons resolve to keep up my spirit if possible. Our little Daughter Seems very heavy and Dull to Day. N.B. I had been keeping her upon a Low Diet &c, &c, and she has taken three Preparatory Pills. She seem'd feverish at Night. The Colonel staid at home all afternoon and Seem'd more Composed, tho' very Low. Not quite so Lame myself this Evening.

Saturd 6. Easterly wind, exceeding Warm Day. It is Dreadful to hear the Number of Children that are Dieing. Charlotte very Heavy and Dull all Day, not able to hold up her Head. We are exceedingly Anxious, indeed I am quite Miserable from Fears. This afternoon the Enemy had a very grand Review, and keep up a Sort of Fight for two hours, with Horse and foot, taking Possession of all their Neighbouring Hills. It seemed to hurry the Garrison a good deal. The Govr at our house a long time this Day, looking at planns and in Conversation with the Colonel. The Col: and he went to the Castle and Lines afterwards. Some new Work is going on there. Charlotte very hott at Night.

Sund 7. Easterly wind. The Col : up at 4 oclock and out with the Genl, did not come home to Breakfast. Abundance of Children Dies with the Small Pox. Charlotte very bad and sleepy all Day. This is the 2nd Day she has been so ill. On each side of our House and Directly opposite three very fine children have Died since Yesterday after being 9 Days bad. Serjt Grant's little Girl died this Day of the Small Pox, about the 9th Day. The kind of Small Pox now chiefly going is a very Dangerous one. Doctor Baynes seems to think our child will get it now, indeed it seems an absolute Certainty as it is in every House in our Street, and in the opposite Door. The Col: and Mr Holloway Dine at Capt Vignolles. Charlotte very ill

in Evening. A Flagg of Truce from Spainiards today and a parley
from them yesterday, Just before the Firing. Find myself Unde
the Necessity of forcing all my Strength in order to keep up, as I fea
I shall have a call for all my Exertion. Towards Night the Chil
grew Violently bad and inclined to Startings. I greatly fear for fitts
She keeps calling for me chiefly. She was Bath'd in Warm Water.

Mond 8. Easterly wind. Charlotte had an exceeding bac
Night and is quite Delirious to Day. Dr Baynes has no doubt of it
turning out the Small Pox. In the Evening We observed some Spott
coming out, and she grew more cool and composed. She is kept ir
the Air, and Drinks Cold Drink, chiefly Toast and Water.

Tuesd 9. Easterly wind, very Warm Weather at this time. The
Enemy very quiet. Our Child going on in a good Way. Seems as i
she would have a good sprinkling, tho' Doctor Baynes says they wil
be of a good kind.

Wed 10. As the Enemy was tolerable quiet now and as Nothing
very Essential occurred, I was not so Anxious to set down every little
Movement which they made in loading or Unloading Small Boat
which were Daily going backwards and forwards to the Orange
Grove. My chief attention is now to my Dear child, who thank Goc
goes Well on.

Thursd 11. Going on well, but very sore, and bad Nights, Still every
thing appears well. She was very patient, tho' in a good deal o
throbing pain.

Fryday, Saturday and Sunday. In the Same Way. Her Night
very Restless, Notwithstanding her taking opiates. On Monday the
were at the height and highly Inflamed. On Wed they all turn'c
and on Fryday took Physick. All the next week continued doing
Right and had hardly any Second fever which is common upon the
Turn. Everything was over even to the last of her Physicking, anc
she was put into a Bath of Warm Water and Herbs upon Saturday
Evening 20th May. We have great Reason to be thankful for thi
Blessing; as during the Course of this last fortnight, not less than 4c
Children have Died of this Dreadful Complaint; and also Soldiers,*
and the air is now quite full of the bad Infection. A very Dangerous
fever is also in the Garrison. All this time Every Means have been
tried to obtain the Gov^rs Leave to Innoculate, but to no purpose.
Every Body appears Unhappy, and are Dreading the approaching
Warm Months. Not any fresh Provision comes near us now; Sc
that we are badly off indeed.

Sund 21. Easterly wind, a fine Day. I went out to the Mount
with the Child for the first time. It was a very Warm Day. Took
a Ride after dinner to Europa. Drank Tea at the House in Town

---

* The two-volume version of the diary says "More than 50 English
Children have Died and Several Soldiers besides Inhabitants."

The Col : not very Well Just now.   A Man of the Artillery fell down 21st May
at Europa and Died as they were bringing him into Town.   Several 1780.
Gentlemen here in Even.   My Maid Eliz^th Dixon taken not well.*

Mond 22.   Easterly wind, fine Day.   Took an Airing to the Southward after Dinner, with Mrs Phipps who return'd to my House.   My
maid ill, but as We had all the Reason to suppose she had the Smail
Pox some years agoe, so we had not any fears.   Abundance of people
ill with the Small Pox.   Every Day 5 or 6 Buryings, and every body
Alarmed and Unhappy on that account.

Tuesd 23.   Easterly wind.   Charlotte quite well.   The maid much
Worse, a high fever.   Doctor Baynes is as attentive to her as he was
to our own child.   The Col : out in Evening.   Not well myself.

Wed 24.   Easterly wind.   No fresh meat kill'd in the Market.
Doctor Baynes pronounces the Maid's Complaint to be the Small Pox.
Great Uneasiness on that occasion.   Thinking she had had it long
before, therefore she was no ways prepared.   We put her into a most
charming airy apartment.

Thursd 25.   Easterly wind very Strong.   We are greatly Distresst
in our family.   The Young Woman very bad.   I am particularly hurt
at it as she now wishes She had been Innoculated.   I am too much
distresst to keep any publick Journal.   Indeed it does not become
Necessary, as most things remain in the same Unpleasant Way, the
Spainish Admiral doing his Utmost to keep up the Blockade.   However We sometimes get In a Boat with a small supply.   Every thing
at this time as Dear as ever ; nor is there any method taken to have it
otherwise.   The Govr says he has not any objection to have the Fresh
Meat as dear as possible.   It is not very easy to know his Reasons
for it,—Contradiction only !   We kill'd a fine sheep this Day ; sent a
Qr to Genl Boyd.   The Rest was used in our House.   We had
Company the Rest of this Week.   We are now obliged to kill a sheep
when ever We wish for Fresh Meat ; which is not of half the Use to
the family as it would be in Cooler Weather.   We therefore now
Exchange with General Boyd's family, each of us having Settled it
not to kill Sheep together.

From *Thursday 25th of May to Thursday 1st of June*, Nothing
happened in the public Way.   Our Servant Maid is past all Possibi-
lity of Recovery.   Every Means is try'd but we find it will not Do.
Men, Women, and Children Dieing every Day and the Utmost
Distress now appears in every Body.   The air is full of this Cruel
Infection.   It is to be wished that the Innoculation had been allowed.
That would have stop'd this Weeks agoe.

June the first.   All the Same Dreadful Situation in our House.   I
did not Stir out.   Our Clergyman, Mr Logie Died about this time.
The Weather most Violently Hott.

   * At the end of the MS. volume is a full journal of the progress of
this maid's illness.

Fryd 2nd. Easterly wind. The whole Family indisposed and i trouble. The Colonel went to the Mount, and staid to Breakfast Colonel Trigg's, also He Dined there ; a very great change in th Maid for the Worse, just at half past one. N.B. From that instar there Remained no possibility of saving her, as she continued in Dieing State.

Saturd 3. Easterly wind. Still Worse and Worse. Find myse very Lame. Baynes here as usual. At Noon she Seemed going, bu Recover'd again.

Sund 4. Easterly wind. King's Birth Day. The Govr receive the compliments of the Garrison upon the Grand Parade at Guar Mounting,—42 Guns Fired at one oclock, and all the Field officer the Staff and the Navy Din'd with the Govr in his Garden. This wa all the Ceremony observed on this Day !

At 20 Minutes before 3 all was over with our Maid Servant, upo the 15th Day from her being taken ill. It is a Most Unwelcom Circumstance and has greatly affected the Colonel ; I am not able t tell what I experience. I was exceedingly ill and hardly able t move.

Mond 5. I went out to the Mount, took the child and Mrs Roger staid there till Evening. She is quite hearty and well ; Seems Muc to Miss her Maid and says she knows what has happened. She is ol enough to know all that has pass'd. Charlotte was five years old i March.

Tuesd 6. Westerly Wind. Bustle and hurry in the House an many Unexpected Difficulties occurr'd, particularly relating to ou Servants. In the afternoon the Col : sent to our Servant Man Jame and Discharged him at that time ; the Man's children were in th Small Pox.

More and More bad accounts of the fatal Effects of the Small Po and Many Severe things said in consequence. It cannot be Wonder' that the Lower Degrees of People should be much hurt at all thes bad times, their Provisions so bad, Nothing to be got to assist then or their poor familys, and the Losing so many fine children, has bee a heavy Stroke upon them, but We hear that a great Person in th Garrison says he thinks it a fortunate Circumstance to those Soldier who have Large familys to Lose three or four Children !

Wed 7. This morning at half past one the Garrison were alarm'd b the appearance of some Fire Ships coming over from Algezira. Th Drums beat to Arms ; and the Garrison fir'd from every part of the Lin Wall where they advanc'd. There was 9 in all. Most fortunatel for Us the wind faild and they were obliged to light these Ships Soone than they meant. They were all driving towards the back of th Rock. It was a most Grand tho' Alarming Sight as they burnt wit great Violence. It seemed to me just so Many Moving Mountain of Fire ! Every Regt was at their Alarm posts and it was generall expected the Enemy would Fire from their Lines. I little expected ^{7th June} such a Shock but I believe I am not Born to partake any very ^{1780.} Common Fate ; otherwise I must have long since ceased to Exist, considering all I have experienced. My heart now seems totaly full of Concern and Vexation ; my bad State of Health has rendered me Miserable. Nothing but Women Servants about me. The first Moment of the Alarm the Colonel went away from the House. To hear the Drums beating, the Noise of the Guns from the Garrison and all our Ships, together with the bursting open of the port holes in the Fire Ships, was beyond the powere of my Pen to express ! I was actually Stupid with Fright,—and at that Dead time of the Night also,—and Circumstanced as I and this whole family were then,—it realy was Distressing. I was even then glad to think it had not happened a few Nights before ; as it would have added to our Concern if the poor Woman had been Sensible of the Circumstances. 6 of these Fire Ships ran on our Rocks and 3 were drove behind the Mountain and got away. Our Men of Wars Boats and the Ordnance Vessels behaved remarkably Well and very Cool. The Vessels continued to Burn all this Day. The *Enterprize* was the first who gave the Alarm of their coming as it was the Guard Boats from that Frigate which Hail'd the Spainish Boats which Were coming with the Fire Ships. The English officer ask'd what Boats and Vessels ? they answer'd Beef Boats from Barbary ! He told them He did not credit it and Instantly went on board the *Enterprize*. The Frigate fir'd one Gun, and not being answerd, they Fired as quick as they could, upon which the Enemy Set Fire to the 7. There were 2 at a considerable Distance, but had no Effect. The bustle lasted till near four and then the Regts were all Dismiss'd. It rained Smartly about 7 which greatly pleased Us ; but the 2 Largest Fire Ships continued on Fire all the Day. One was Drove near to Rosia Bay where the *Panther* Lay, and got In between her and the Shore. It was very Evident the Enemy meant to set fire to the *Panther* and to the New Mole. Thanks to Providence They were Disappointed. May they always be So. I was, as well as many others, much affected with this unexpected alarm. Col: dined out. Mr Holloway with me.

Thursd 8. Westerly wind. All quiet from the Enemy. Find myself greatly indisposed and very Low all Day. Had a little particular Conversation with Mr Holloway,—not of any use after all.

Fry 9. Westerly wind. Still very Low and ill. Two or three boats arrived from Tangier, brought letters and News papers. N.B. Not any for Us. *The Man's* child Died.

Saturd 10. Westerly wind. All the Same in the Camp &c. Very ill. Settled to dine at Mt to Morrow.

Sund 11. Westerly wind. It began to Rain about 8 in the Morning, continued to do so till Noon. It then cleared up and I went in the chaise to the Mt. Was very ill when there and could not Walk

11th June, 1780.

out. Return'd at Nt. A good many in evening. 2 Market Boa
from Tangier ; Beef and Mutton.

Mond 12. Westerly Wind. All quiet in Camp. Worse and Wor:
in the Small Pox. Have had 3 exceeding bad Nights and am still i:
Take a Ride in afternoon to Europa, took 2 Miss Phipps who Drar
Tea with me.

Tuesd 13. Easterly wind. All the same Uncomfortablenes
The Enemy took a Setee* coming over to Us with Provisions. N.l
This was contradicted afterwards. Not very Well.

Wed 14. Easterly wind. Find that all the Ships are gone froi
Algezira and that Barcelo has Hoisted his Flagg on board a Xebequi
He went behind the Mountain last Night. I wrote this Day to m
Son and to my Sister.

Thursd 15. Easterly Wind. The Ships attempted to sail last)
but was obliged to Return as the wind came about. I therefore ser
an other letter by Mr Colvill to my sister. N.B. Those I wrot
yesterday went in a public packet from the Convent, in a Boat t
Farro. Colonel Green has also sent letters by Col Gledstanes, as
did one to Capt Nicolls by Capt Ormsby who went in the same Boa
with Gledstanes. The 3rd Mate of the Highland Regt Died.

Fry 16. Easterly wind. The Boat made an attempt to go bi
was obliged to return. Col : at Dinner at Col : Ross.

Saturd 17. Easterly wind still. Changes making in the 12th an
73rd Regts. I write a long letter to Capt Nicolls and sent it by Caj
Ormsby. He has sold to Lt Colt of 73rd for twenty four hundre
pounds. Capt Mackintosh's Lady (73rd) Died suddenly this Da'
Colonel Gledstanes goes home as is said upon account of his ill Stai
of Health. Grow very ill in the Evening and quite Lame. M
Cuppage call'd here in afternoon.

Sund 18. Easterly wind. The Boats not gone. The Col
Breakfasted at the Mt. I went in the forenoon to pay some Visii
in Post Chaise, and afterwards to Dine at the Mt, Return'd i
Evening.

Mond 19. Easterly wind, but not Strong enough to take out tl
Boat. Col : at the Mt in afternoon to meet the Genl. A mistake i
some Money Matters ; the Col came home in very good spirit
having had a pleasant Walk with the Genl. Find myself not very wel

Tuesd 20. Westerly wind. Very Warm now. The Colon'
Walking in King's and Prince's Lines with the Gov' to Day. H
dined at Convent, Mr Holloway with me. Some Spainish Enginee:
seem'd Busy on the Beach taking a Survey. A Boat arrived froi
Tangier brings Word that the Spainiards had taken an English Vess(
bound for this place from Under the Guns at Tangier. This hurts i
a little. Find myself ill at Nt.

* A small sailing vessel.

Wed 21. Westerly wind. Col breakfasted at the Mt; Busy about taking in some more ground to Improve, dined at home.

Thursd 22. Easterly wind. Dull looking Morning. Go out to the Mt after Breakfast, take Kitty Phipps, went to the Hospital, dined at Mt and came home in even. This Day it was in Orders that the Assisting Engrs and officers employ'd as assisting Overseers should be dismis'd upon the 24th Inst. Boats for Farro go this Evening, and a Leghorn Ship, on board of which was Mr Colvill.

Fry 23. Easterly wind. Find that one of the Boats for Farro is gone, and also the Leghorn Ship. Col Gledstanes and Capt Ormsby went in the Boat; Mr Colvill in the Ship. A Boat is going away to Farro this Evening, call'd the *Fox* belonging to Merchant Andersen by which I wrote a letter to My Sister; and sent it to the Convent, being resolv'd to try all opportunities. Hear that the Enemy is making some kind of Defensive Work upon their Coast, which looks as if they were alarm'd for themselves. A small Boat arrived this Day from Minorca, left the *Porcupine* Frigate there, brings Word that the Garrison was under some fear of being besieged, and that they had no Supplies from any where. This Boat brings news of Some Gun Boats coming down here from Majorca.

Saturd 24. Westerly wind. This Day at Noon Several large Xebeques and one Frigate came from Ceuta, and in a very Impertinent way came near the New Mole. The *Panther* and *Enterprize* fir'd and the *Enterprize* sufferd from the Blowing up some combustibles on board, 15 men Wounded. I went to Mount Pleasant at this time, with an Intention to Remain out for some time, my Health being very poorly and I am willing to Try every possible Means to be Well at this Sickly Miserable Period. Came up in very great Dejection of spirits, fear I shall soon feel the fatal effects of it. Greatly is every family hurt at the Daily Misery of the poor Dieing Children.

Sund 25. Easterly wind. Settling myself at the Mount. Heard no News.

Mond 26. Easterly wind. All pretty quiet. Many Boats now at Algezira. Am very ill all Day.

Tuesd 27. About half past one this Morning we were alarm'd by a Firing in the Bay. I got up, and my Windows at the Mount afforded me the Means to See much more of this attack than I expected or Desired. It was from Boats of a particular Construction, of which indeed we had Received a Sort of Information from Minorca. They each Contained one Gun and a Large Number of Men. They evidently were attempting to destroy the *Panther* and the Ships in the New Mole. It was exceedingly dark at the first and as they were low in the Water could not be distinguish'd except from the Flashes of their Guns. The *Panther* was Laying in Rosia Bay (the same station as when the Fire Ships came) and her Stern was towards the Boats when they first fir'd. She afterwards changed her situatior trying to bring on a Discharge from her Broadside. The frigates an other ships fir'd as did those Batterys that bore upon them fror Bonna Vista, New Mole, Rosia, and every where was possible to b of any use. The 2 Regts that were at the South Barracks turn'd ou the firing continued till past 2. We could now tell with certainty th Number of Boats. Some of their shot came on Shore. One fe between the Vineyard call'd Picardo's Garden and the South Pavilion one very near to the Centinel at the Grand Magazines. As the Da advanced they all disappeared. They are very Low in the wate: By 4 oclock all was over ; and no hurt done at all. We were a a good deal Alarm'd. From this time and for many Nights after w were constantly alarm'd by shot firing ; sometimes by the Frigat mistaking the Watch Boats, sometimes from the Enemy over a Algezira, and this Month of June ended in Nightly expectations (More Boats, as it was now well known they mean to burn or destro the *Panther* but we hope they will not Succeed.

Saturd July 1st. All quiet from the Enemy. Find myself growin exceedingly indisposed. Nanny Redway came to our Family.

Sund 2nd. Still ill ; pains seemingly coming on ; and a grea Weakness all over my whole Frame ; The *Second* Child Died—ver sorry. Number of Signals from over the Way, and all observed wit great exactness by the Camp, Queen of Spain's Chair, &c, &(Between Sunday the 2nd and Monday Morning the *Panther* saile It was not in the least Suspected, but no doubt was in consequenc of those Gun Boats having so plainly shew'd their Intentions t Destroy that Ship. On Monday Noon a Row Galley came over fror Algezira and plainly discover'd the *Intent*, which was to look if th *Panther* was in the Mole or if actually gone. It was Universall believed that Admiral Barcelo was on board in a Disguise. The came by much too near and in a very insulting Manner parade about. It was plain to be seen that a person in a Fisher Mans Dres was the whole time looking through a Spy Glass ; as Many of ou officers were doing the same. He seem'd to be making particula observations, sometimes standing up. This Person was either Barcel or some officer of Trust. Our Frigate and an other Vessel fir'd a the Galley. She kept Her Colours up the whole time and when sh had sufficiently amused herself went off. A Night or two after thi More Boats came over. It was pretty clear at their first appearanc and I plainly discover'd 6 Gun Boats. We fir'd very heavily at then and they had Repeated Signals made from Algezira and from Poin Negro &c which they obeyed, and after being about an hour in th Bay disappeared.

The Rest of this Month little Essential occur'd. The Same Ur easiness proceeding from the Blockade. The Enemy are tolerabl quiet at Nights, only taking care not to allow any thing to go out o

to come In to Us. Provisions are dreadfully Dear and exceeding 2nd July
Scarce. Very bad for Sick Families. 1780.

Tuesd August 1st. Easterly wind. Had a very bad Night, the
pain intolerable in my Hip and Back. Send In to the Col: who
informs me that Baynes has promised to come out in evening, that
the Col was to dine with Col Picton. Battle of Minden Day, cele-
brated by Col Picton, 12th Regt. All Ended in perfect Harmony.
Col: came up in evening in very Easy Temper; Baynes came. In
great deal of pain all this evening. Dinah came up likewise, ill with
a pain in her Head and face. The wind came Westerly about Nine
oclock and Blew hard. Great scarcity of Provisions. About this
time Major Horsfall of 72nd sold his Cow for Fifty Guineas and a
pint of milk every Day !

Wed 2. Westerly wind. Had a very painful night, could not stir
myself. Take some of the pills for the first time. The Col : did not
come out this Day. Betty went into Town in the Evening as George
is not well.

Thursd 3. Westerly wind. Still exceedingly bad. Dinah had a
Blister &c. About Noon We observed at the Gut's Mouth a Sort of
Engagement between some Galleys and a Large Boat or Setee.
However they were so distant We could not tell, but it is too much
fear'd it is the *Fox* pacquet Boat. Whatever it was they have taken
to Tangier we think or to Cadiz.

Fry 4. Westerly wind. A Setee got In with great difficulty from
Minorca. She was closely follow'd by Row Galleys. She brings a
Small Supply of Wine, Honey, and a few pigs. We hear about this
time that the Ports in Barbary are totaly shut against Us ! The
Moors will not shew the least inclination to assist us. On the
contrary they allow our Vessels to be taken in their Harbours. This
We learn by Means of Several Parleys which have come In of late
and in particular of an English Vessel's being taken a few Days agoe
as she was going into Tangier, that the Passengers are gone to
Algezira and that there is among them an officer of the 56th Regt
and a Merchant and his Wife who are to be sent in a Flagg of Truce
in a few Days.

From this Day till Saturday the 12th nothing particularly Worth
Mentioning occurr'd.

Saturd 12. Westerly wind. Just after our Morning Gun Fir'd
there were Signal Guns and Rockets fir'd from Caberitta point and in
half an Hour a Brig appear'd coming round the point. She was
chased by 4 Small Galleys. She fir'd two Guns to Us by Way of
Claiming our Assistance. She was Directly known to be a Brig
belonging to Merchant Mackellar, call'd the *Dolphin*, from Lisbon.
He has long expected her, is Loaded with Wine, Oil, Sugar, &c.
The same Vessel had been a long time in Tangier Harbour and has
been twice fortunate enough to get In here with Supplies. She now

<table>
<tr><td style="vertical-align:top; width:20%">12th August,
1780.</td><td>saild In with a fine wind at the Day break.   Unluckily it faild at ha
past 4.   She made for Europa.   There our Batterys fir'd and fro
Bonna Vista, but not one shot hit the Galleys.   We fir'd one Sh
from the New Mole Head to encourage her.   She came at last ve
near our guns, and We flatter'd ourselves she was out of Danger,
the 4 Small Galleys seem'd Shy of our Batterys.   At this Insta
2 very Large Row Galleys came pouring down from Ceuta.   Th
encouraged the others, so that to the Universal Concern of the who
Garrison they Boarded Her.   She would not Strike.   I saw the whol
Manoeuvres from the very instant she first came round, saw all H
sails shot away, the Grape Shott flying all over her Rigging.   Th
last shot carried away her Lower sails and Yards, then it was easy t
Board Her, and I plainly saw the first Spainiard get on Board, it
impossible to express the discontent of the Garrison on this occasio
The Enterprize was in the Mole, but every Body expected all th
Boats would have been arm'd and sent out, which if they had whe
the first signals were made from the point it is beyond all doubt w
should have got Her Safe In.   It certainly is the most Unpleasa
Circumstance that has happened to us, and has occasioned Man
Severe things to be said against our Navy Folks.   No Wonder.   W
dread to hear the fate of the Captain and Crew.   They must ha
Suffered We think.   She Lay to for half an hour after they took He
and as it was a Dead Calm and she was much hurt they Tow'd h
over to Algezira.   It is supposed to be an Essential Loss to th
Garrison as we are in Want of every Commodity which we know s
had on board.   Mr Mackellar says it is a very great Disappointmen
He hopes his share was insured.</td></tr>
</table>

(To be continued).

A LADY'S EXPERIENCES IN THE GREAT SIEGE OF GIBRALTAR (1779-83).

BEING THE DIARY FROM 1ST JUNE, 1779, TO 13TH JUNE, 1781, OF MRS. GREEN, THE WIFE OF LIEUT.-COLONEL GREEN, CHIEF ENGINEER OF GIBRALTAR (AFTERWARDS LIEUT.-GENERAL SIR WILLIAM GREEN, BART., CHIEF ENGINEER OF GREAT BRITAIN, 1786—1802). EDITED BY COLONEL E. R. KENYON, R.E.

(Continued).

Sund 13. Westerly wind. We find every Body full of anger and Vexation from Yesterdays business. I came into Town to dine and by desire of the Col am to come In to remain till the great Heats are over. I return to the Mt at Night. 13th August, 1780.

Mond 14. Westerly wind. The Flagg of Truce not appearing !

Tuesd 15. Westerly wind. The Flagg came about Noon. The crew of the *Dolphin* Brig is arrived too and all safe except one man who had his arm broke by a splinter. The men in the Boats were not very civil to them, but Admiral Barcelo was exceedingly kind to them, at the same time expressed his Wonder that our Boats had not been sent out. He made the Captn a present of 70 Cobbs and told him He was under the Necessity of putting down in his Journal of what Prizes was taken by them that this Brig was taken within Gun shot of this Garrison. The officer of the 56th is come over, and the Merchant as they call'd him proves to be a Mr Hamilton, Husband to the Woman who was hurt in the Leg by the only shott which has as yet come Into the Town from the Enemy, on Jan the 12th. The Woman who is also come over, proves to be the sister of Mrs Hamilton, Widow of Serjant Gray of the Artillery, a smart Looking Person who says that Admiral Barcelo was exceedingly Polite and kind to her. She had several letters for this Garrison but they were all taken. The officer did not Lose any of his Baggage. The Vessel was coming Here with Bale Goods and many Necessaries for different Merchants here, had only been 11 Days from Plymouth. All this seems to add to the Distress of the Garrison. One only Comfort is that the Small Pox seems to be Dieing away. Indeed it was Dreadful to hear the Daily Losses. More than 500 have Died. The Smallest Number has been of Soldiers, as there has not been more than 50 Died, but their poor Families are greatly thinned, and their Grief is great at not having been allow'd to Innoculate. It might have saved the Lives of Scores. Therefore it is a very great Distress to think of this Misfortune.

th August,
So.

The 16th and 17th I remained at the Mount. The weather Violently Hott. Nothing particular pass'd in these Days and I came into Town on Friday 18th in order to Remain some time. The Weather very Close and Uncommonly Warm. Find myself rather Lame in Evening. Mr Cordoza Died. Col Mawhood taken Dangerously ill.

Saturd 19. Westerly in the Morning. Violently Warm. Find great pains in my Limbs. At Noon there seemd an Easterly wind. It proved so and Blew hard in the Evening. 2 of our Men of Wars Guard Boats went off last Night to the Enemy, 16 Sailors on board !

Sund 20. Easterly, Dull and foggy. Am not quite so Lame as yesterday. The greatest difficulty now to provide for a family. We got as a very great favour 20 chicken this Day, 27 Dollars, and 12 Ducks for 20 Dollars. This Day continued exceedingly Warm and Close, Col Mawhood very bad. Our 2 Gun Boats went out in Evening. We had been firing at the Enemy's Boats from our Batterys at Europa and drove off two Galleys. One who had been Driven in too close in the Nt and had come to an Anchor was obliged to leave it behind.

Mond 21. Easterly and Foggy as Yesterday. Find myself quite Lame and affected by the Weather. Go to Capt Phipps in Evening. Cheese is now 1 Dollar the pound, sugar 1 Dollar, and any tolerable tea 6 D^{rs}. This Day there was a meeting at Mr Power's House. A Remarkable dinner this Day, given by Col Ross in part, he sending an English Sheep to the Master of the Assembly House. It ended in great Noise and Riot. The Company was not very Numerous, only 21 Gentlemen.

Tuesd 22. Easterly wind, Close and still Warm. Find myself rather Worse for being out last Night. Mrs Gray Here to Day. Had some few Gentlemen to dinner. An English Shoulder of Mutton from Mr Power. I mention that from the Rareity. It was in exchange for something We had to spare. A pretty Large party in Even. Every thing now growing Dearer and Dearer.

Wed 23. Easterly and foggy. Very Lame to Day, could not get up to Breakfast. The Articles of War was read to the different Corps this Day. Upon the Parade of the 39th something very dis-agreable passed. The Lt Col, Colonel Ross, went there Under a Visible agitation ; after the Regt was Drawn up He ask'd if Genl Boyd as Commanding officer of the 39th was upon the Parade. He was told Not. He then order'd the articles to be Read, after which to the surprize of every body He address'd the officers and soldiers, talking first of the True Meaning of those articles and afterwards attacking the Colonel of the 39th calling him Bob Boyd, and the Regt the Storekeepers Regt, and said a vast deal tending to hurt Genl Boyd in the Eyes of the Men ; and He also order'd the Adjutant to tell the Genl all he had been Saying ! but as He declin'd it one of the Genls Aid de Camps did. It is Supposed this will occasion much Confusion. Colonel Mawhood is thought past Recovery. He is as bad as possible. He was only taken ill with a Complaint in his Bowells upon Thursday the 17th inst. He had dined at a Wager Dinner given by Col Picton upon Tuesday the 15th. The Night before had been at Phipps, and the Evening after at Major Fauncourt's, and this Complaint came on very suddenly. He took some trifling things of himself at first, but sent for his own Surgeon directly, and Dr Baynes also was with him upon the Thursday, so no time had been lost. This afternoon it was the most Uncommon Heat that has been for many Years, Therm^r at 93½ and at 10 at Night, 82. 23rd August, 1780.

Thursd 24. Easterly. Close and foggy as yesterday, tho' not quite so Hott. Very Lame this whole Day. Every Body is full of what pass'd upon the 39th Parade. Mrs Rogers with me this afternoon. Col Mawhood as bad as possible. Col Ross put Under Arrest this Evening by Lt Genl Boyd. The Small Pox seems now quite over.

Fry 25. Easterly wind. The Line of Battle Ship left Algeziras this Day and went towards the West. Barcelo fir'd three times this Day on account of its being St Luis, the Name Day of the King of France and Princess of Asturias. Find I have got great cold coming in my Head.

Saturd 26. Easterly wind. Blowing hard all Night. The Col Breakfasted at the Mt. I did not go as being Unable to get up. Col Mawhood alive but totaly given up. Col Ross in Orders for a General Court Martial on Tuesday Next. Colonel Green President, 1 Lt Col, 5 Majors, 6 Captains ! This Day a small Vessel (or rather Boat) arrivd from Minorca in a few Days, brings very few supplies or News. The Govr has a few things sent as a Present from Genl Murray which He says He shall send to the parade to be sold by auction and will not be a purchaser himself. The Govr has a Declared dislike to having presents made to him. Indeed He is very little Try'd that way. It will be rather hard if He makes it a point with officers that may fortunately have a family Necessary sent to them, at such a scarce time as this. It is to be supposed He will change his Mind on that Head. Col Mawhood still alive but in a Dreadful Way.

Sund 27. Hardly any wind. Violently Hott. Col Mawhood still alive ; and tolerably Easy. Col Green had a Tooth Drawn this Morning. This turn'd out rather a pleasanter Day with regard to Heat than any of late. I did not stir out, not being as yet well enough. A good deal of discontent arising about this Court Martial, particularly between 2 of our Captns of Engineers ; (one being in orders for a Member) and it came to Captn Evelegh's turn. He pleaded his being Aid de Camp, but as there never had been an overslaw ordered for him it was impossible to avoid returning him to

27th August, 1780. the Adjt Genl. However the Govr instantly ordered the overslaw ! and Capt Phipps was to Sit.

Mond 28. Westerly wind. Warm Morning. Col Better ; and I went down to Breakfast. Colonel Mawhood has had a bad Night and is going into a very bad Alarming Way, Something nearly Despairing &c. This morning 2 young officers of this Garrison, Mr Stephens of 39th and Mr Johnson of 56th went out to the windmills in order to settle an Idle business, merely the Effects of their being Young Men. They were parted ; and the affair is to be Settled by Commanding officers. A more Serious Matter passed upon the South Parade yesterday morning between the Govr and Lt Col Making. This Evening Doctor Baynes call'd and acquainted Us of the very bad way Col Mawhood was In, and telling Us it was not possible for him to hold out many hours. He had made two Alarming Attempts, proceeding it is supposed from Delirium,—one, of some *Nails ;* one of a Bathing Tub—Every body is concerned ; as He is a very Worthy Man and exceedingly well Bred and Gentlemanly in every Respect. He has not been well from the first of his coming to the Garrison in Jan.

Tuesd 29. Westerly wind ; the Col getting ready for the Court Martial. Capt Pigot of the 56th had wanted to sit in the Room of Capt Price of that Regt ! It was an odd desire, but had been complied with Yesterday ! However this Morning it was changed to the first orders, and the 6 Captains were positively settled as follows,— Capt Phipps, Engineers ; Capt Eyre, Royal Artillery ; Capt Perryn, 12th Regt ; Capt Price, 56th Regt ; Capt Lindsay, 73rd Regt ; Capt Shand, Royal Artillery. The above is according to Dates of Commissions. The Court consisted of Colonel Green, Lt Col Craig, 56th ; Major Fancourt, 56th ; Major Hallows, 56th ; Major Dawson, 58th ; Major Horsfall, 72nd ; Major King, 58th ; and the six Captains. Col Mawhood died this morning, was Open'd at Night. A Mortification in his Bowels had taken place, and likewise a Stone as large as a pistol Ball was found in his Gall Bladder. It was no wonder He had been long ill and oppress'd. As the Doctors agree, He could not have been in any Health or Spirits for a long time past.

The Court Martial assembled at 10. Colonel Ross went attended by Lt Col Kellet, Major of the 39th, and the Adjt of the Regt. Lt Genl Boyd went in his Lt Genls Uniform with his Aid de Camps. The Court went over for the Day at 2 oclock. The same two young Gentlemen that went out Yesterday, went out again this Morning, attended by Seconds. Mr Stephens Pistol shot away one of Mr Johnson's Waistcoat Buttons and part of his Shirt but did not hurt him.

Wed 30. Westerly wind. This Morning a Small Boat, with 5 Men, came over from Tangier with a packet from Mr Logie to the Govr containing very Unwelcome News ; by which we learn that all

Communication between Us and Barbary is Stop'd, and in Con-
sequence We cannot expect any Supplies. The Court Martial Meet
again. Col Mawhood Buried this Even ; the Ceremony as follows—
The whole 72nd Regt with their Colours and Arms as usual on such
occasions, Under Major Horsfall's Command. They form'd a Lane
from the Colonel's House to let the Corpse pass through. The
Gov' was Chief Mourner, his four Aid de Camps walking first, the
Adjt Genl and Qr Mr Genl on each side of the Governor, Every
officer off Duty in the Garrison. Lt Genl de La Motte walked at
the Head of the Brigade of Hanoverians. The Pall Bearers, Colonel
Green, Colonel Picton, Colonel Godwin, Lt Col Cockrane, Lt Col
Trigge, Lt Col Mackenzie, Lt Col Craig, Lt Col Kellet, all with
Crapes round their Arms, and all the 72nd with crapes, which they
wore about a fortnight afterwards. N.B. Many Ceremonys were
expected, but for what Reasons were omitted no Body can tell ; it
not being as yet known who had the Direction of the whole, tho' in
part it is Guess'd at. Genl Boyd was not there or at the Court
Martial to Day. Capt Lesley of the *Enterprize* Frigate paid a very
handsome compliment to Colonel Mawhood Corpse, as He had
Minute Guns fir'd from the time The Body mov'd to its being Buried,
and all the King's Vessels had their Colours half-staff. The Colonel
was Buried at Southport ! It was expected he would have been
in the Church.

Thursd 31. Easterly wind. A Close Damp Day. The Court
Martial meet as Usual, and it was expected that Colonel Ross would
have come upon his Defence, as He had begun on that head yesterday. He was then desired to say if he chose more time, but He said
He was perfectly ready. However this Morning He had changed his
mind, and after reading a long paper and Relating some past Circumstances respecting an old Regtl Coat which He had Worn for these first
2 Days of the Court Martial, and which was only to bring In what
passed between Himself and Genl Boyd 5 years agoe ; (for so long has
a coolness subsisted), He then desired the Court to indulge him for
two Days. As that would bring it to Sunday He was told the Court
would therefore adjourn to next Monday. N.B. He was Dress'd
properly this Day and told his Reasons for not having been so the
other two Days. Genl Boyd was not there. It is much to be wish'd
that things had not been brought to this length. It is hardly to be
suposed they will now ever be properly settled. It is the opinion of
many that Colonel Ross would rather chuse to have this Dispute
settled in a more *personal* Way. It is so much more Deeply Fix'd as
it has been so long coming on, and on the Col's part seems a total
Disregard and a poor opinion which He has thought proper to form of
the General, who in course has shewn himself the Commanding
officer of the 39th, in fact there seems a fix'd Mutual dislike,—and it
is realy a pity. N.B. I have omitted as yet to mention the charge

given in by Genl Boyd. It was that Colonel Ross had spoken disrespectfully of Genl Boyd at the Head of the Regt and had shewn an Intention to hurt the Genl in the Eyes of the Officers and Soldiers of the Regt, as his Discourse tended to that purpose.—I may not be exact as to the Words, but the above is the Substance. N.B. It was by every Body thought a very Mild charge, all things Considered, as there was some parts of the Colonel's Discourse that evening at the Regtl Parade that might have turned greatly to his own Disadvantage.

Fry September 1. Easterly wind. Dull Close Morning. The few remaining Vessels that We had were expected would sail as last Night, but they did not. People begin now to be very Uneasy in the prospect before us, and it is much to be feared that the Troops will show their discontent. It seems almost impossible for any Ships to get out as the Enemy have a constant Line of Boats and other Vessels from Ceuta to Caberitta.

Saturd 2. Easterly wind. More and More Complaints about fresh and Salt Provisions &c. Veal has been sold at 10 Rials the lb. We gave to Day 3 Cobbs for the Qr of a Hill Kid which weighed a little more than 5 lb. One fortunate thing is a great Quaintity of Fish are now brought In almost every Morning, which is a great comfort to the poor men and families.

Sund 3. Easterly wind. Exceedingly Warm Close Weather. The Colonel Breakfasted at the Mount, as did Charlotte and two of the Women. I did not go. Find myself very Low and dull and still Lame. Had a Leg of Veal to Day, $12\frac{1}{2}$ lbs at one dollar pr lb ! Upon the whole every one seems uneasy. A man of the Artillery Died rather Suddenly. He only went into the Hospital on Saturday, and Died this morning. Inflamation in his Breast. We had some Gentlemen in Evening and in Conversation I heard of a circumstance which I had never been inform'd of by the Col: which was that the Gov[r] had accepted Some Grapes from Mrs Godwin and a Melon from Major Barlow. It so happen'd that Col Green was present at both the times when the Gov[r] thank'd those Gentlemen for their presents, but at the Same time he Seem'd to look rather Confused when he found the Col was close to him. N.B. Oranges.

Mond 4th. Westerly wind. The Court Martial meet again. Col Ross was Dress'd and appeared cool,—said he Did not mean to Depreciate Genl Boyd " but only to put him to his true Standard ;— just as We do to Good or Base Metal. We always chuse to prove our Coin,—if it turns out of pure Gold in its quality it is the more Esteem'd—from having gone through the Trial—but if otherwise, We know it and always look upon it as Base Metal."

The above and Many other such like Speeches He made. He very freely and openly confess'd that He had said all and every thing which had been mentioned by all Genl Boyd's Evidences such has having call'd the General "Bob Boyd—For he knew the Genl was a man of Humour and liked to be free with his Superiors; nor could He conceive any harm in calling the 39th the Storekeepers Regt, as every Body knew Genl Boyd had been a Storekeeper." N.B. When Genl Boyd, on the first Day's Trial (the only one of his being present) gave in his charge or was examin'd He seem'd a great deal affected and said it was hard for him at such a time as this to appear as a prosecutor against his Lt-Col, but He beg'd leave to observe that He Glory'd in having been Storekeeper, that He had Carried Arms long before He had the Honor of being either Storekeeper or Judge Advocate, and He thought himself a very fortunate Man when he was appointed to those two Departments. Genl Boyd refused a Seat which was offer'd him. ^{4th September, 1780.}

The Sentence of Court Martial—A Suspension of Twelve Months and render'd incapable of ever Serving in the 39th Regt. The Governor took off Nine Months of the Suspension and mitigated the Later part ! This seems a pointed partial business and has rather Hurt the Members of the Court Martial. Every person seems more or less affected at this and the Regt seems very Uncomfortable. The Court Martial is again Sitting, upon a Soldier of the 58th for taking charge of an other Soldier's Musket as he was standing Centinel at the South. The other man is an Hanoverian and has been detected some Days before in Stealing some Money from one of his Mess Mates. He ask'd the Man of the 58th to hold his piece just for a Moment. This it seems is often done. But He made to the Line Wall, with an Intention to get over, was there stop'd. He is to be Try'd by their own Law. Our Man is one of exceeding good character and is well liked by all his officers. The Sentence is not known.

Wed 6th. It rained this Day for the first time this Season. It Cool'd the air. The 17th Hundred part of an Inch of Water fell. The Court Martial was dissolved this evening. The Colonel much indisposed. Very large Straw Heaps now made up, by much Larger than Ever,—and also over at Algezira. We had a very fine Hind Qr of House Kid from the Coxswain ; for which We paid 1 dollar a pound ! The Qr Weighed 9 lb.

Thursd 7. Westerly wind. Col not at the Parade. The Man of the 58th was Brought down at Guard Mounting in order to hear the Sentence of the Court Martial ; which was to Receive 500 Lashes, but in Consideration of his good character He was recommended to the Govr by the Court and He was in consequence forgiven. Colonel Ross is put out of Arrest and made acquainted with the Sentence of the Court Martial. N.B. No Sentences are ever put into orders, and this is the first that has been made any way public since Genl Eliott came to the Garrison.

Fry 8. Westerly wind. Close Morning. A Man of the 39th Received 300 Lashes upon the Grand Parade this Morning for attempting to Desert. In the course of last Night 2 men of the 56th deserted. The Col rather better, changed his apartment yesterday. He took a third of James Powders in the evening. He had a good night. His room is next the Garden and is a very Delightful Airy Bed Chamber.

Sat 9. Easterly Wind. Col not at the Parade. Very Busy all of Us in Moving the things from out of the Drawing Room into the Large New Room. Find myself a good deal Dejected and Low in Spirits. A great deal of talk of the Govʳˢ Management Relating to the late Court Martial as he has Undertaken to alter it in all points. A Bomb Proof (which was begun in the Month of August) making under the Garden in the Town Quarters, is in good forwardness. It will be a very useful place in case any Bombardment takes place ; it is done by Diging under the Garden ; which is very high above the Level of the Street. The opening is just opposite our Dining Parlour, in the Front Court. It will consist of three apartments, and it Runs deep In. In the further part, near to the Coach House Yard (which is also next the Street) is an apartment just long enough to hold a small platform and has a Window, large enough for a man to get through which may be Useful in case of any quaintity of Rubish should come into the Court Yard. The Top of this Bomb proof is cover'd over with many well prepared coats of Hardend Clay &c &c well Ram'd down and finish'd as Usual with such Buildings. It is about Nine feet Thick. If this is never Wanted as a Bomb proof it will be capital Cellars. It has added to the Look of the Front Court, opens with 2 Doors, between which are two Bulls Eyes ; and the Doors are folding ones. It has a very good appearance. It is a Work of much Labour, attended by plenty of Uncommon Noise, Raming down, and Corking, all amongst the Heavy Oak Timbers &c. The Noise is not of any Consequence ; when we think how Essential it may be hereafter. It is so handy by being near the Colonel's House, by affording him the means to throw In his papers or whatever else He wishes to have at hand for his Use. N.B. A Number of Signals made last Night from Admiral Barcelo and from the Camp and Queen of Spain's Chair. It was the whole Night long.

Sund 10. Westerly wind. Fine Morning. All pretty Well. The Colonel not at Grand Parade. He took a second dose of James Powders, which I increased to half a paper. It had no effect till near five in the Morning and it then threw him into a pleasant Perspiration ; and he slept till near 8. He seems tolerably well now. He went to see Col Ross this forenoon ; all well.

Mond 11. Westerly wind. Col at Grand Parade had an Unexpected and Unwelcome Conversation with . . . about Some Workman belonging to the 58th who was employed not where it was Supposed. The Col was totaly Ignorant of it as the man had been discharged from the King's Works since last March. He spoke his Mind very freely to . . . This I am sorry for, as I fear may occasion some Unpleasant Consequences, for I am certain it hurts a Man of the Colonel's temper. It has brought on a good deal of Uncomfortable Conversation amongst the Engineers and has agitated the Colonel. He has spoke his mind very freely to Evelegh. I sincerely wish it had not happened. This evening the Battalion of Saboya went from the Camp and Several Baggage Wagons had brought Parcels from Algezira like Beding &c, and had returned from the Camp with the Same kind of Baggage. *[11th September, 1780.]*

Tuesd 12. Easterly wind. The Col at Grand Parade ; all tolerably quiet. We fir'd a shott or two from Middle Hill at a Boat that was coming too close In. We see that the Enemy have hung some men In the Camp to Day. I am not very well. This is the Anniversary of our firing upon the Enemy, but all has remained quiet from them.

Wed 13. Easterly wind. The Colonel went up the Mountain Early this Morning and Breakfasted at the Rock Guard with a Party of Artillery and Engineers, Captns Loyd, Martin &c. This Day the Bakers were allow'd to bake only a certain fixed Number of Loaves each,—according to an Order given by the Govr. 5 Quadruples given this Day for a Calf ; each qr will weigh about 20 lb. Loaf Sugar is now Nine Rials to the lb—Powder Sugar 7Rs. Tea that used to be 4 Dollars is now 6—and all in proportion Dear and Scarce.

This is the Meeting of American Gentlemen belonging to that Club, to celebrate the Memory of Genl Wolfe. Colonel Green President.* It consisted of 21. All Concluded exceedingly Moderate and Agreable and the Col came home before 7 in evening. The Party which breakfasted at the Rock Guard also Dined there—all except Col Green who came down to the Dinner.

Thursd 14. Easterly wind. A Setee arrived in 20 Days from Minorca. She brings a tolerable Supply of Wine, Oil, Sugar, and Hogs—a few Turkeys too. But all these are to be disposed of Under Certain Restrictions and of course very dear. No one is to be allowed to buy more than one of each kind ; such as one Pig or one Turkey &c. A General Court Martial Sitting this Day. Major Barlow of 12th President—upon a man of 56th found sleeping upon his post.

Fry 15. Easterly wind. The articles of family Necessaries that the Boat brought down from Minorca are to be Sold this Morning at Water Port. We get one Pig, it is small ; will weigh about 10 lbs the Qr. We gave 22 Cobbs, viz., 33 Dollars. This Day 2 Battalions from Algezira March'd to the Camp with flying Colours &c.

Saturd 16. Easterly wind. Nothing very particular in the Camp this Day. The Soldier who was Try'd on Thursday for sleeping on his post Received 500 Lashes this Morning on the Grand Parade.

---

* Col. Green had been wounded at the capture of Quebec.

Sund 17. Westerly wind, pleasant Morning. All Quiet. I went out to pay a few Morning visits,—called at Mrs Goding whom I had not seen for a long time. All well.

Mond 18. Colonel not very well. A few Tents are pitched near the first River.

Tuesd 19. Westerly wind, fine Morning. A Party of Ladies Breakfasted at the Rock Guard! I can not boast of being of that *Military* Set,—and afterwards din'd at Poca Roca Cave. Some Beef in the Market to Day, 6 Rls pr lb.

Wed 20. Westerly wind. The Enemy are working at Some kind of Sand Work on this Side of their Lines, between two Batterys which they formed some months ago. It appears like making a Drain. There is an other Regt come into Camp. All remain quiet as yet. A Parley came this Day and brought a letter from Don Martin Alvarez to the Gov relating to some family letters belonging to Captn Vignoles of 39th and which the Spainish Genl assured our Gov and Captn Vignoles should most punctually be sent In if they ever should fall into their Hands, as they Solely related to a Sum of Money left by his Father to Him. By this Parley we hear that the *Fox*, pacquet Boat, was taken at the time We Suspected it and that her Master and Crew were to come In in a few Days.

Mrs Gledstanes dined with Us. Colonel Mawhood's Auction of Goods &c began as this Day when every thing Sold at an Amazing price. N.B. I must observe that at this time when every family article is so Dear the Exchange is at 38 pence the Dollar, which makes it still a higher price for every article. The cheese is one Dollar per lb—chickens 15 Rials a piece, pigeons 20 Rials a pair.

Thursd 21. Westerly wind. All quiet in Camp. Colonel in the Evening at Genl Boyd's. I seem to Understand that Colonel Ross is highly displeased with the Sentence of the Court Martial, as thinking it a very Severe one. Also so Does Many of a Set in this Garrison who are partial to their Country Man! This afternoon Captn Shand and Mr Seward of the Artillery got leave to Walk out at Landport. The Second Day of Col Mawhoods Sale of Goods. It is astonishing how the Books and any Article sold—meerly it would appear as if it was because they had been Colonel Mawhoods! N.B. The Gov and Genl Boyd had been allow'd to take their first Choice of Books. The Gov also thought fitt to take all the Maps. They were Good ones.

Fry 22. Westerly Wind in the Morning. Col: at Mount and Charlotte Breakfasted with him. This Morning the Enemy began to Dismount some of their Guns at the Artillery Park. They have several Working Parties. At Noon the Wind came Strong Easterly. No sort of Notice taken of this Day being the Coronation. Find I am growing much indisposed and am fearful it will increase. Quite Lame. A Squadron of Horse came into the Camp, supposed by their

Uniform to be the (left blank in the diary). A Parley to Day and 22nd September, 1780.
one Return'd.

Saturd 23. Easterly wind. Hear all the remaining Ships are expected to sail this Night. I write. a long letter to my Sister, as did the Colonel to His son and two Letters to Mr Fisher ; one of those last letters went in a Brig belonging to Merchant Anderson—the others and Mine to my Sister went Under Care of Mrs Gledstanes. A Flag of Truce came over this Day and brought a Midshipman who had been taken off one Night about a Month agoe by the Men who went off in a Guard Boat belonging to the *Enterprize.* Some Sailors also came and they all bring an account of the Spainiards having taken a Large Number of our Store Ships ; belonging to a West India Convoy ; and carried them into Cadiz ; and that We had taken 4 of their Line of Battle. This Day a Calf was killed for which the Butcher gave to the owner 140 Dollars...£21. It is to be sold at 10 Rials per lb...4s$^{s.}$ 4$^{d.}$! the Pluck with the Heart at a Pistole...15$^{s.}$ 6$^{d.}$ A Butcher this Morning offer'd to give £200 for 4 of the Oxen employ'd in the King's Works, and 2½ Guineas are given a piece for Young Pigs of 6 weeks old. In fact it is not easy to tell the impositions that are Daily made upon the Army by those Inhabitants who have any Live Stock to sell ; nor is it possible to tell the Distress of the poor sort and of the Married Soldiers. The Great Want now seems firing. There is plenty of Flour thank God, but the Wood is So Scarce that the Bakers are not allowed enough to Bake as Much as formerly. The poor Women and children are round the Bakers Doors every Morning, in Vain Waiting with their money. Tho' they have Money they cant get Bread. It is hard upon those people. The Troops of Course Eat their full allowance of Bread. It is their familys who feel the hardships and are to be greatly pitied.

Sund 24. Westerly wind. Not any Ship able to go out. I have been exceedingly ill all Night, a most Violent pain in my Left Arm and ill in all Respects, did not stir out of my Bed Room all Day. A Red Flagg has been hoisted on board a Frigate at Algezira 2 Days. N.B. A Court Martial.

Mond 25. Easterly wind. All quiet in the Camp. Am a very little Easier. A Cow belonging to Capt Uniacke 58th pretty far advanced in Calf fell down from some part upon Wind Mill Hill, was either Dead or obliged to be instantly Kill'd, for which He Received 300 Dollars in Money and a Milch Goat Valued at 30 Dollars. This Beef was Sold at 7 Rs per lb. Dollar 38 pence. N.B. It is now said that Capt Uniacke had sold this Cow to the Milk Man some Days before this accident happened. If so the loss to the poor Man was very great and it does appear better on the Captn's Side. He really did receive the above Sum &c for the Cow but no doubt the Milk Man expected the Calf would live.

Tuesd 26. Easterly wind. Looks like Rain. Find that some of

<table>
<tr><td>6th September, 1780.</td><td>the Ships got out last Night, viz., the Dutch Ship Handalein and the Brig belonging to Mr Anderson. It was the Ship with Mrs Gledstanes that sailed. I am rather better this Morning but not Well enough to go down stairs &c. The Colonel had a party of Gentlemen to play cards in evening. It is to be a sort of weekly meeting.</td></tr>
</table>

Wed 27. Easterly Wind. 2 more Ships got off last Night and there are still two remaining which I hear are expected to sail this Night. On board of one goes a Mr Young and Wife by whom I write to my Daughter Nicolls. Find my arm better, but very ill.

Thursd 28. Easterly Wind, but to our Disappointment these 2 Ships did not sail. It seems they can not go Unless they Receive Orders and it is to be feared they will now be too long Detain'd. It was one of the most favorable Nights, blowing very hard and Dark. We are all much Vex'd at this Delay.

Fry 29. Easterly wind. A Deserter came In this Morning, a Serjt of the Wolona Regt. He came upon his Hands and Knees from the Lines! He brings a Confirmation of the Enemy having taken our West India Convoy and that there are 59 Vessels now in Cadiz. The Men of War that was the Convoy are got away We hear. A Spainish Frigate came from the East, very much disabled, having Lost Her Bowsprit &c. N.B. I omitted to set down the Orders of Wed 27 "Biscuit will be delivered in Lieu of Soft Bread from Monday next the 2nd October till further Orders, to begin at the Boat House. Hospitals to have Soft Bread."

Saturd 30. Westerly wind. A Boat getting ready for Minorca. Much talk about this Deserter. He is by Birth a Strasburger, has been in Many Services, Speaks English, was four years in England carrying on a Sort of Trade. He is Suspected to have come In more as a Spy than any other Thing. He has the Dress of a Peasant on ; says He sold his Regtl Sword and watch to purchase it. He is a very handsome clever man. The Govr has sent him out to the Southward and has order'd that a Noncommissioned officer should go everywhere with Him. This afternoon We had the Vexation to See a Ship taken Into Algezira which is believed by most Judges to be that one with Mrs Gledstanes on board ! We had flatter'd ourselves she was got clear off. Suppose We shall hear more about this to Morrow. The Deserter also reports that the Enemy have a Work all Ready Fram'd ; a Sort of Battery which They intend to bring through the Lines the first suitable Night. They have it seems been waiting for Dark Nights ; and it is now such.

At the Close of this Month all Degrees of people begin to look Uncomfortably, and it is much to be feared the Unpleasantness of the times will rather increase than lessen.

Sunday Oct 1. Westerly wind. This Morning at Day Break it was discovered that the Enemy had been busily employed and had Erected

a Sort of Battery near to the Tower upon the Neutral Ground, con- _{1st October,}
siderably on this side their Lines and about 700 Yards from the _{1780.}
Bayside Guard. At Day Break they also Set Fire to the Garden
Hutts, Destroying the Wheel belonging to the Well. At the Same
time they advanced and fix'd a Sort of Combustible in form of Hand
Granade and other Inventions upon and standing against the Pallisading
at our Inundation, amongst our Out Guards. As Soon as the Centinels
observed this they began to Fire, but those at Forbes Guards seem'd
to be alarm'd and came in to Landport. Those at the Head of Kings
Lines were very alert and fir'd all their ammunition. N.B. Some of
these Fire Works were inclosed in Skins and as big Round as a Man's
Body. Others were Smaller and were with an Hook all Ready to hang
upon the pallisading. The Large ones were set against the pales.
Some were also done up in Tin Cases, Cover'd over with a kind of
paint ; to hold the Lighted Matches. Captain Martin was upon the
Batterys ; did not hear any thing of the Enemys Manœuvres till it
was Day Light. It is every Bodys opinion that they will Fire as Soon
as We begin with them. Therefore it is now more Resonable to be
fearful than ever it was. The Work they Erected last Night is at
present of no use to them, but it may be only by Way of Commencing ; or to divert our attention, or to provoke, and draw on, our
Fire. However it has put Us all in Motion, and most of the officers are
going up the Mountain. Captn Loyd went up to Relieve Captn
Martin at Guard Mounting. Col Green three times up the Rock this
Day, went to the Govr at 2 oclock. Articles of War read this Day.
I shall be better able to Speak more on this Subject very Soon as I am
promised to have a full account of what the Enemy has done and where
about this Battery is Erected. It is about 100 ft in length and pretty
thick. The Bomb proof Under our Garden is nearly Completed. It
is quite ready now for Use. In Consequence of what has happened
We put a few Necessaries In lest the Enemy should attempt any
thing this Night, as it is believed We shall throw a few shott at
them. We therefore get ourselves pretty Well Guarded. About 8
this Evening Captn Loyd threw some Light Balls. He could not
distinguish any Persons at the Work, or hear any Noise. We
continued throwing those Balls till near 10, then Left off and again
began at 2 in the morning. The Enemy did not return our Shott.
We are now certain that is the Vessel with Mrs. Gledstanes on board
and an other that went out the Same time she did. Mrs Gledstanes and
her 5 children &c was plainly seen through several of our Glasses this
morning as they were removing Them from the Ship. Every Body
is concerned at it. She took a letter from our Govr desiring if she
should be taken that the Spainiards would forward Her and family to
Farro or Lisbon, informing Them she was a Field officer's Wife who
was gone to England some months agoe upon account of His bad
Health. We all hope such a letter will lead Admiral Barcelo to shew

proper attentions to Her and that He will Send Her to Cadiz rather than back into this most Wretched Garrison. The Guards mount at 8 and the Gun Fire's at 8 in the Evening. We Seem to Understand that Conde D'Estaing is come or Daily expected over the Way and in the Camp, as the last Flag of Truce, one of the Spainish Genls *Aid de Camps*, told our Sec^ty that He was expected upon a Visiting footing to the Encampment. He has been at Cadiz Some time ; and as We hear, is to have his Flag on board a Spainish Man of War and is to act Under Don Luis de Cordova.

Mond 2. Westerly wind. All quiet from the Enemy. About 6 this Morning a very Large Suite of officers came down to the Spainish Lines, amounting to 40 with Guards &c. It is Supposed to be D'Estaing. The Party went to Fort St. Philip. This forenoon we had the Mortification to see 2 other Vessels taken into Algezira ; it was the Dutch ship that has laid Here a long time the *Handilein* that should have gone out the Same Nt with Mrs Gledstanes ; and one other Transport. This makes 4 that have been taken over there. N.B. Andersons Brig We hope and believe is got off Safe to Farro. There are Several English officers on board those ships, most of them Gentlemen who have been changing from out of the Regts in Gib^r,—A Mr Gregory of 58 and a Lt Cook of 56th. At Noon this Day, as the Suite returned from the Lines to the Camp there was 17 Guns fir'd from Point Negro, which Seems to Confirm the opinion of D'Estaings being there. Our out Guards are Order'd to be particularly attentive. They are So ; and fir'd Small Arms in the Course of last Night from Bay Side. The American Club Day—very Moderate indeed. Colonel Ross was upon the Grand Parade this Morning at Guard Mounting for the first time Since the Court Martial. He had his Sword on. Made Several Visits afterwards, call'd upon me in the forenoon ; Looks Well but seems a little agitated and rather Grave.

Tuesd 3. Westerly wind. Very early this Morning the Enemy was observed to be Working at their New Battery. The Govr sent Word up to Fire upon them. They did So and a great many Shott and Some Shells were thrown. We dislodged some part of the Work but did not do any Essential Hurt. They keep a few Men and a Centinel there the whole time. The Garrison now seems in a Bustle and the following was in Orders this Day,—" In case of any Sudden Attack in any of the Posts the Officer Commanding there will make such Disposition for the Defence of his post as the nature of the Attack may seem to him to require." The Govr was up at Williss before Dinner, and as We hear pointed one of the Guns, which had the Good luck to hit their New Rais'd Work. N.B. If this is not true I will mention it in my Journal as a mistake.—N.B. A Mistake. At three oclock a parley came from the Enemy Relating to Sending In those soldiers wives and other Women that were taken in those Ships that are now over at Algezira. We also hear that Mrs Gledstanes is to come which We are all very sorry for, and think it hard indeed upon her. 3rd October, 1780. At 4 a Memorandum was put into the General Garrison Orderly Book as follows,—" As the Govr expects Count D'Estaing will Reconnoitre the Garrison in a Boat the Officers Commanding the different posts are not to Fire at Him except He comes too near, but in that case are to fire over Him." The 2nd of the Whist meetings at Judge Frazers. N.B. Several Persons who saw the Party Yesterday Seem to think it was not D'Estaing but Conde de O'Reilly who is Captain General of the Province of Andalucia. Time will let us know more of this matter.

Wed 4. Westerly wind. Major Burke went out with an answer to the Enemy's Parley of yesterday. He went on much further than Usual in order if possible to give a Glance at their new Work. The Guard which was there call'd out to him, making Signs not to advance, but He Seem'd not to hear. He was just able to give one Look at the Rear of the Work. It is totaly Unfitt for Service as yet. The Flag of Truce is to come In to Morrow. A Privateer Cutter was taken last Night in the Bay, coming from the West and carried into Algezira. A great Number of shott was fir'd on both sides. A Xebeque took her. A small Boat came late this Evening from Barbary; no kind of Supply; only 2 letters from Mr Logie to the Govr.

Thursd 5. Easterly wind. A Parley this Morning came In by which We find that Mrs Gledstanes and her family are to Remain at Algezira till an answer comes from Madrid. This pleases Us much more than if she was Sent In, and is no doubt in consequence of the letter which she carried from the Govr. The other Women are to come In today.

Fry 6. Westerly wind. All very quiet this Day. In the Course of last Night I was taken Violently ill, with a Dreadful pain in my Leg, attended with a Fever. Continued in Bed all Day, and at Night much Worse.

Saturd 7. Westerly wind. Worse than before, grew so bad that Doctor Baynes was obliged to Bleed me on Saturday Evening, not able to be taken out of bed. I was engaged for this Nt at Major Fauncourfs but sent the excuse. The Flag of Truce came In. We hear the Admiral Barcelo is exceedingly polite to Mrs Gledstanes. This Evening it Rained most amazingly hard; and at 4 the Sunday morning and on till 7, it was Violent. We hear D'Estaing is gone from the Camp to Cadiz.

Sund 8. Westerly wind. Raining hard indeed, but no harm done. Three Inches and half of Water fallen in the course of last Night and this Morning. It cleared up at 10 and was a very fine Day. I was rather Easier but could not be taken up. The pain all in one Leg, can not get any Rest or Sleep, very Low in spirits. What English officers were over at Algezira are gone with D'Estaing by sea to Cadiz.

Mond 9. Westerly wind. Find myself a little Easier ; get up for the first time about one oclock. It Rain'd a little this afternoon. Ill at Night. Great complaints of the Dearness of every article ; one calf killed which Sold for 10 Rials pr lb ; and one Pig for a Dollar per lb.

Tuesd 10. Westerly wind. All Quiet this Day. Am a little Easier, get to my Work again. This Evening the Col Went to the 3rd Whist meeting at Col Craig's. He was *here* before He went. My Spirits exceedingly bad and not to be Wonder'd. Disappointed in many things, particularly Dr Baynes.

Wed 11. Easterly wind. Raining a little this Morning. We hear of a Minorca Boat coming In who Mentions a Vessel Seemingly one of a Dutch Convoy going to the Enemy from Malaga, being behind the Rock. Our Boats went out and We had the Satisfaction of bringing Her Safe In. She is Loaded with Many Useful Articles ; says he is a Dane. The Master appears Sulky and Seems Uneasy at coming In. Some people doubt if We shall get the Fruit or Oil or indeed any thing from on board. She Certainly did not Mean to come In, only was Drove too near. Several Row Boats were after Her. The Weather very mild all Day.

Thursd 12. Easterly wind. Find myself exceedingly Low and ill and that it is absolutely Necessary to change my Room for the Air. I came out into Dressing Room on Crutches. A man of 56th Deserted from Signal House Guard. He got as far as the Devils Tower quite Naked. He was fir'd at from Williss with Grape Shott. He got behind the Tower. At last upon Seeing a Boat going Round he took Courage and ran across the Sand to the Nearest Centinel of the Enemy, who Received him, and got into the Lines in Safety. The Vessel which came yesterday is not Dutch We are now convinced, is loaded with Oranges, Lemons, Raisons and Figgs, which We hear is to be sold here. The Boat has brought Some Oil and Sugar, also some Cheese. It Rained a little This Day. There is not to be any more Parleys by Land on either Side for the future ; all by Flag of Truce by Sea.

Fry 13. Easterly wind. Raining this Morning. Close Damp Weather. Affects every Body more or less. Of the Number of Complaining Persons I am the foremost as I am at this Instant so ill and so hurt in my Constitution that I can not Walk. Out again in my Dressing Room, very helpless, can not Stand but on Crutches.

Saturd 14. Easterly wind. Dull and Close. Still very helpless. The Lemons and Oranges are this Day sold to those who gave in their Names to the Q.M.G. In consequence we got a Double Chest of Lemons. They Seem very fresh and Good. It is said they will come Reasonable, tho' the True price is not known as yet. The other Articles are not to be Delivered till next week. We have got some of the Cheeses from Minorca and are in expectation of oil. This Day there is a Calf Selling. The Veal is 10 Rials. That indeed has been the price of late, but it exceeds all beleife almost ; when I add that

I0 Dollars was this Morning given for the Head and Feet ! the Pluck 14th October
sold for 6 Dollars. The Butchers are begging any officer or Person 1780.
who is in possession of Cows or Sheep to part with them ; and the
price they offer is beyond all idea. 12 Guineas a Butcher offer'd our
principle Servant Man for one of the Colonels Sheep, and £60 for one
of the oxen in the Kings Works, both which, of course, Were Refused
by the Man.

Sund 15. Easterly wind. A very great Fogg early in Morning
which clear'd up about Noon, and it turned out a very Close Warm
Day. I try'd to go down to dinner but could not. Several Persons
call'd. Col : at the Mount with the Gardeners. 2 Gun Boats belonging
to the Enemy Rowing about in the Bay all Day. N.B. I am to get
a Drawing of one of those Boats.

Mond 16. Easterly Wind. This Morning early one of our Batterys
at Europa fir'd a few shot at the Enemys Gun Boats which were
coming too close In. They afterwards fir'd at a Boat of ours ; on
board of which was Lt Burleigh of the 39th Regt who has an appointment from our Govr as Commanding a Party of Marksmen to be Ready
on Certain Duties. He was out this Day fishing. The Shot went
over his Head and Struck against the Line Wall. He brought it into
the Garrison. I had a Visit this Day from Genl Boyd—all very Well,
very Sociable. Lt Holloway of the Corps of Engineers has been for
some Days employ'd Laying a Large Boom at New Mole,—a Work
of Labour and trouble. I got help'd down to dinner this Day.

Tuesd 17. Easterly Wind. Colonel at the Mount to Breakfast
with the Gardeners. The Enemy again firing at our Garrison fishing
Boats, particularly the Hake Boats. They are, and have been, very
busy at a Work, just on the other Side of their own Lines, but of what
kind is not quite Certain. They do not Seem to go on with their New
Work on our side the Lines—that still remains in an Unfinish'd
State—it is supposed to be intended for a Mortar Battery.

Wed 18. Easterly Wind. A Cold Uncomfortable Day. The Gun
Boats out again, and Strive all they can to hinder our geting Fish,—
however We still get some, tho' of course it will be attended by this
Consequence—the fishermen will avail themselves of this New diffi-
culty, and encrease the price of Fish, which is already exceeding Dear.
N.B. The Salt fish is quite over—that is amongst the Troops. N.B.
No Sorrow Shewn on that Occasion.

Thursd 19. Easterly Wind. A Boat arrived from Minorca. No
live Stock. Some little quaintity of Wine and Sugar. More Gun
Boats, which We fire at from the different Batterys and from our Ships.
The following Orders given out this Day :—" Issues of Provisions for the
next Month, commencing 23 October and ending 19th Novbr 80. The
Stoppage of Beef will be paid for at the rate of 20 Quarts per pound—
whereas by the agreement last Janry the price was settled at 12
Quarts ; and the Oatmeal at 24 Quarts per Gallon. Bread as Usual.

19th October, 1780.

Officers pr Month. 6 pound of Beef; 4 pound of Pork ; 4 pints of pease ; 6 pints of Wheat, 3 pound of Flour, 2 pound of Raisons, 4 pints of Beans (in lieu of 12 pints of pease and 30 oz of Butter) ; 10 oz of Butter ; 4 pints of Oatmeal ; 4 lb of Beef, 8 pints of Oatmeal (to be paid for).

N.B. Colonel Green continues to Draw his allowance of Ten Rations.

Men pr. Week. $1\frac{1}{2}$ lb of Beef ; 1 lb of Pork ; 1 pint of pease ; 1 pint of Oatmeal ; $2\frac{1}{2}$ oz of Butter ; $1\frac{1}{2}$ pints of Wheat, $\frac{3}{4}$ lb of Flour, $1\frac{1}{2}$ lb of Raisons, 1 pint of Beans, $\frac{1}{4}$ pint of Vinegar (in lieu of 3 pints of pease and $7\frac{1}{2}$ oz of Butter) ; 1 lb of Beef, 2 pints of Oatmeal (to be paid for).

Hospitals pr week. $1\frac{1}{2}$ lb of Beef ; 1 lb of Pork ; 3 pints of Oatmeal ; $2\frac{1}{2}$ oz of Butter ; $1\frac{1}{2}$ pints of Wheat, $\frac{3}{4}$ lb of Flour, $\frac{1}{2}$ lb of Raisons, $\frac{1}{2}$ lb of Rice, 1 pint of Beans, $\frac{1}{2}$ pint of Vinegar (in lieu of 4 pints of pease and $7\frac{1}{2}$ oz of Butter) ; and 1 lb of Beef (to be paid for).

Fry 20. Westerly Wind. Colonel Green went on board the Several Ships in the Mole and Harbour and Examined the Boom at New Mole. More Gun Boats. It is now known for Certain, the Enemy have put down a great Number of Anchors near where our Boats go fishing. Time will Show what They Mean by it. This Day remarkably Warm for the Season. Every Body wishing much for Rain—both on account of Peoples Health, and likewise for the Gardens—that being of very Essential Consequence just now. The Gov[r] has given part of that Ground at Landport call'd the Govrs Meadow to Some of those poor men who Suffer'd by the Enemys Burning their Gardens and Hutts.

Saturd 21. Westerly Wind. A Boat is bringing Round from Catalaine Bay. She is coming to Us from Algiers ; Loaded with Wine and Leather. Many People thought she would be put Under Quarantaine, but it was not So. N.B. The *Enterprize* Boat had been on Board before any of the Garrison Boats, and the Govr had Received Some Letters. Quarantaine could not therefore be so Well observ'd as that would have Subjected all *Parties* to share alike. This Evening a Number of very Large Ships appeard in Sight from the West—all Line of Battle. They appeard Under Russian Colours. Yet Many are of opinion They are French Ships, going most likely to Touloun. They went through the Gutt towards the East. There were 8 in all.

(To be continued).

A LADY'S EXPERIENCES IN THE GREAT SIEGE OF GIBRALTAR (1779-83).

BEING THE DIARY FROM 1ST JUNE, 1779, TO 13TH JUNE, 1781, OF MRS. GREEN, THE WIFE OF LIEUT.-COLONEL GREEN, CHIEF ENGINEER OF GIBRALTAR (AFTERWARDS LIEUT.-GENERAL SIR WILLIAM GREEN, BART., CHIEF ENGINEER OF GREAT BRITAIN, 1786—1802). EDITED BY COLONEL E. R. KENYON, R.E.

(Continued).

Sund 22. Westerly Wind. Clear fine Morning. The Colonel and Child went to the Mount to Breakfast. The Setee from Algiers is safely come Round. The Enemy were at their New Work last Night. The Captain upon the Batterys did not hear them till pretty far on in the Night. He threw some Light Balls and one Shell, but the Balls were Instantly put out ; either by Water or Sand. In the Morning it was Seen how Large a Quantity of Sand they had thrown up in Front of the Work. The Govr went in the Forenoon to Williss and orderd two Shells to be thrown at 10 this Night and Light Balls frequently. This forenoon a Barge with a Flag of Truce came from the Enemy. Capt Vallotton, as first Aid de Camp, went from the Govr in the Cutter to Receive the Message &c. It was a letter for the Govr. The Gun Boats have been exceedingly Bold and Impertinent all Day and at 3 oclock 4 of them came within Gun-Shott of the Shiping in the Mole &c—fir'd at the *St Fermin* Frigate and our Shiping ; and at the Garrison too. We return'd their Compliment and fir'd Several Balls from 32 prs on the Kings Bastion and from South Bastion &c. One of the Shott from Kings Bastion went through the Sail of one of the Boats. They were Drove off in about half an hour and did not return any more this Evening. A Shott from one of the Gun Boats came on Shore at the Clay Pitt at South Shed. It went 5 feet Deep into the Solid Earth ; the Serjant upon that Work had the Shott taken to the Kings Yard. It Weighed 26 lb (a Spanish Arrove). An other of their Shott also came against the Line Wall near the Shed where some Provisions are kept but did not do any harm. A Death at the Convent, after two months Sickness, and Buried at South Port—21 Years Old.

Mond 23. Westerly Wind. Fine Day. All Remained quiet last Night. The Flag of Truce was a letter to inform the Govr that Mrs Gledstanes and family were Safely arrived at Cadiz and had every Civility paid Them. More Gun Boats all Day.

22nd October 1780.

<table>
<tr><td>24th October,
1780.</td><td>

Tuesd 24. Westerly Wind. An exceeding Warm Day. Every Body wishing heartily for Rain. The Colonel up at Rock Guard and afterwards breakfasted at Williss with Captn Loyd ; had an opportunity of Seeing every Manœuvre of the Enemy, as the Morning was Uncommonly Clear. This Day the Cask Fruit from on board the Danish Ship is Selling by Auction,—consisting of Raisons, Figs, and Grapes ; the last Article done up in Large Bunches in Sand and in a Jarr ; the Jarrs of Raisons Sold very Dear—some 8 Dollars ; the Jarrs of Grapes sold at different prices. We got an exceeding Good Supply of every Article,—and a Cask of Figs. The oil was uncommonly high pric'd ; the Sallad oil at 15 Dollars a Arrove, which used to be 6 and 7 Dollars, and Lamp oil for Kitchin Use, that was frequently Sold for 2 Dollars we now give 10 and a half for.

Wed 25. Westerly Wind. The Enemy have added Something to their Work last Night. We continue to throw Light Balls, and after that Shells every Night, and also Ball and Grape Shott in the Day time, but it does not Seem to affect them in the least. They are likewise Busy at a Work, seemingly a Strong one, at Caberita point,—and this Day carried away some Guns from their Artillery Park with an Intention We suppose to go to Caberita. We know to a Certainty the Enemy have 80 Mortars in their Lines and at the Camp. It is believed there are already 42 of that Sort at the Lines. I find the Boat will Certainly sail this evening for Minorca, therefore I write a letter to my Sister, as it now is Said to be the only tolerable chance We have. We Understand there is a paquet between Minorca and Leghorn. Several Jews and Inhabitants going. More Gun Boats every Day.

Thursd 26. Westerly Wind. The Boat went last Night. A very fine Day. The New Regulation of officers Provisions took place ; N.B. The Beef is quite Rotten and Stinking. It seems to hurt every Body. The Troops are far from Well ; and to a Certainty are very weak and greatly fallen off in their Strength and likewise in their Spirits.

Fry 27. Westerly Wind. A Cold Raw Day, looking like Rain, but it did not. I had fix'd in my Mind to go out ; which I did in forenoon, went as far as Back of Grand Store. The Enemy have added considerably to the Work on this Side the Lines, and have thrown up a vast quaintity of Sand (a Parallel)— upon each Flank. The Govr has order'd Shells and every other kind of Fire to be sent, according as the officers see them, more or less employ'd. In the mean time our Garrison is very Alert in all Respects and Strengthening in a most Surprizing Way every part, which indeed Seem'd as Strong before as possible. The Number of Traverses is prodigious, and are still adding. It is realy Comfortable (as far as Such a Circumstance can possible be) to See how Much the Safety of the Troops is consulted by the Chief Engineer. The Govr and Chief Engineer Seem

</td></tr>
</table>

wholly devoted to Care and Anxiety for the Garrison. This even very cold. 27th October, 1780.

Saturd 28. Westerly Wind. The Weather very cool ; and Rain in the Evening, but very little. The Govr Here this forenoon and almost every Day. We now fire very much at the Enemys New Work. N.B. I shall make a few Remarks at the Close of this Month with Respect to this Work. A Flag of Truce was sent in a Barge this Day from Us—which was answerd by a Barge from the Orange Grove. It began to Rain at 10 at Night and continued till one.

Sund 29. Westerly Wind. A very Cold Raw Morning, and afterwards turn'd out an exceeding Wet Afternoon and Night. The Enemy have last Night and for many past ones added to the New Battery—Notwithstanding all our Firing.

Mond 30. Westerly Wind. More Work done last Night. General Boyd here in Evening having first been with Col Green to the Montague Bastion where some New Experiments were try'd,—Firing for the first time from Montague Bastion—it seemed to hurt the Enemys New Works.

Tuesd 31. Westerly Wind. Two men Deserted from their post from Upper Alls Well*,—one of the 39th the other of the 56th. The Captain at the Lines did not make a very Regular Report of that, or of our firing &c &c to the Governor. It is thought He will receive a Severe Reprimand. A Large Number of Vessels going through to the East—supposed to be a French Convoy.

At the End of this Month all Degrees of people begin to be Uneasy at the total Silence that We are cruely obliged to have with our Friends.

The Work that the Enemy began to throw up and was discovered upon the first of October was a Front Epaulment with two returns at right Angles, advanc'd upon the Isthmus, about 600 yards before their Established Lines.

On Oct 2 we in our turn Now added to our Works by making the Great Traverse on the North Bastion the Basis of the Parapet of a Cavalier for four Guns. This and Several additional Strengthenings towards the North part of the Line Wall were Laid out by the Chief Engineer.

Wed November 1. Westerly Wind,—raining and very cold. The Enemy making every addition they possibly can to their New Work on this Side the Lines. We fir'd Shells and Shott from Montague Bastion last Night and frequently in the course of this Day. A Man of the 56th deserted. It makes every Body Uneasy to find the Spirit of Dissatisfaction beginning to encrease amongst the Troops. Most of the Regts are affected, more or less, with the Scurvy. About this time we had several of the Large Tunny Fish brought In.

* This is a post above the eastward end of Princes Lines.

2nd November, 1780.

Thursd 2. Westerly Wind. Cold and Wet. The firing much the Same on our Side. We know that Some of our Shott and Shells have taken Effect, as our people upon the high Batterys frequently hear the Groans of the Enemy, and likewise We have Seen them this very Morning carrying away Several Wounded Men upon Hand Barrows. The Enemy are likewise Busy at a New Work on their own Side of the Lines, as also upon a Strong Work at Caberita point. 2 Large Ships appearing like Frigates are this Day gone over to Algezira—and are supposed to be Loaded with Stores. The following was in Garrison Orders :—" The 56th and Field Marshall Hardenbergs Regts to hold themselves in readiness to Encamp on the Shortest Notice. Upon these Regts being order'd to encamp they will assemble on the Kings Road—Hardenbergs with their Right to the Castle, and the 56th on the Left of Hardenberg's."

Fry 3. Westerly. Cold Morning. The Enemy have been very busy all Night, have made a pretty deep Track from their Barrier to the Tower near to their New Work, but it is not thought deep enough for Heavy Artillery. This morning early two Men Deserted, one of 12th the other 56th. They went off together, got round Under the Line Wall and Swam off it is Supposed, as their Cloaths were found there. This Evening the officer Commanding the Marks Men * went up to Williss and to the Head of the Kings Lines, and fir'd very frequently all Night, as did the Captain upon the higher Batterys. Also we fir'd a good Number of Shells from the *Montagu*. It now is become exceedingly Uncomfortable, for as soon as it is dark the Enemy begin to Work, and of course *We* begin to Fire. Our House is just in the Line of Fire, and we are Shook by every Shott, particularly from the *Montague*—it absolutely Shakes my Bed with Violence. I believe I may add with Truth that there are hundreds keep awake beside those on Duty,—and this is the case every Night. I have not mentioned anything relating to Fresh provisions lately, as it is only to repeat the Same Unhappy Circumstances for the poorer Sort of People, some few only being able to *look* at what little Meat is kill'd,—and that now begins to be only Pork. We believe the Calves are all Kill'd,—the fish too is very Scarce. This Weather is very good for the Gardens.

A Memorandum in Orderly Book.

" When the 56th and Hardenbergs are Order'd to encamp, the 72nd to remove their people Quartered in Town into the Casemates under the Kings Bastion and Montague Bastion. 2 of the 4 Companys of the 12th Regt Quarter'd in Irish Town to be doubled on their own Corps, and the other 2 on the 39th Regt. Genl La Mottes to be doubled on the Pavilions and their own Barracks at the back of the Parade. If it shall become

* See Oct. 16.

Necessary to remove the 3 Companys of the 12th from the head of the Parade, and Captn Loyds Company of Artillery, the Company of Artillery and one Company of the 12th to be Quarter'd in the Casemates under Water Port, and the other 2 in the Nitch's of the Galley House. The officers in the first Instance to be distributed as follows :—Artillery, Engineers, 12th, 39th, Redans, and La Mottes, amongst themselves,— 72nd Regt in their present Quarters. The officers of the 58th and 73rd to remove to the South, and to be Quarter'd with their own Corps. All the Hospitals to be ready to Move on the Shortest Notice."

Saturd 4. Westerly Wind. A great Day this in Spain, being St Carlos, the Name Day of the King. Barcelo and all the Ships at Algezira are Dress't ; and fir'd three times, as Usual on those Occasions. The Track to the New Battery was Deeper this Morning than before. We fir'd very much this Night.

Sund 5. Easterly Wind. Raining very hard at Gun Fire and at Guard Mounting. Find myself very indifferent all Day and not in good Spirits,— had a fire by desire of the Colonel in my Bed Room to Day. Much talk of the Supposed Intentions of the Enemy, as to whether they will come on or not at this time. Every Body seems Anxious to Move to the Southward. The Navy Hospital is to be taken in part for the Garrison General Hospital. Doctor Baynes has reported room enough at this Instant for 400 men, but there are Wards for 1,500,—only some are full of Stores for the Navy. Numbers of the 72nd* dieing every Day. A Meeting of the Corps of Engineers this Day, in consequence of the Orders relating to the Quartering in Case of the Enemy firing,—as all the Engineers are at present quartered on the North Side of the parade except Captn Phipps, whose Quarters are near the Bomb House. The Gun Boats were again troublesome this forenoon, as also in the Evening.

Mond 6. Westerly Wind. This forenoon the.........was at our House and unexpectedly gave a good deal of trouble and Vexation to the *Chief*. It hurt his Temper all Day, and broke In upon his Intentions. The Colonel went to the American Club, but did not Stay longer than half past 4. He then went upon business, and afterwards return'd Home alone, not over well pleased. A good deal of firing all the Evening.

Tuesd 7. Westerly Wind. The Man of the 12th who deserted on Fryday last was drove on shore near to the Convent Battery. He was directly known, and this Morning a Coat was first discover'd, behind the Rock, belonging to the 72nd Regt, with some hard pieces of Bread and cheese in the pockets,—the Coat torn all to Rags. In the forenoon upon making a Close Search, the Body of a Man Dreadfully Broke to pieces was discover'd. He had Undoubtedly belong'd

---

* 73rd in the other copy of the diary.

to the 72nd as the mark upon one stocking shewed. He and 2 others got away near a Year agoe, and it was always Supposed had got clear off. The Way this Body was found makes it plain He had not been of the Lucky ones in Escaping. The Col: is but indifferent all this Day, went to the Weekly Whist Party at Capt Loyd's in the Evening. Very little firing this Day. The Enemy are doing what they think proper to their New Work, in the Day, as well as at Night—Notwithstanding our Shells &c. &c. We kill an English Sheep at this time—use it in our own family ; and exchanged one Quarter as Usual with Genl Boyd. This Evening about 7 oclock there was some firing at Caberita point, and Signals made, which We believe to be in consequence of Some Vessel coming In from the West, and just afterwards a Loud Explosion was heard, and it was judged by many people that a Boat or Some Vessel, must have been blown up,—perhaps one of the Enemys Gun Boats. We continue a a good deal of firing all Night.

Wed 8. Westerly Wind. It is now Certain that it was a Gun Boat Blown up, as there was only 3 discover'd this Morning in the usual place where there has ever been 4, and We can also See an English Cutter over at Algezira. This Morning at 8 oclock, a Man of the Artillery who was Under Confinement in the Provost and had been concern'd in a Robery at Captn Martins and had turn'd Kings Evidence took an Opportunity to Settle the business by Hanging himself in the absence of the Centinel. He was quite Dead—a Young Man about 22 years old. The Enemy have added 3 Good Traverses in front of their New Work, and have Workmen now employ'd in it. Captn Lesley and Captn Falkner and Several others of the Navy Din'd with Us to Day. It is exceeding Cold, but very Clear Weather Just now. The Govr here in forenoon. A Great firing in the evening.

Thursd 9. Westerly Wind. Cold Weather. Find myself very ill. We fire a great deal during the last Night, but the Enemy advance greatly with their New Work.

Fryd 10. Westerly Wind. Cold Raw Weather. The Enemy have taken a Large Mortar from the Lines and sent it away in a Boat to Algezira. Captn Loyd upon the Batterys to Day, and at 8 in the Evening began a very heavy firing. It was at Large Working parties and Carriages. A Boat arrived this Evening from Minorca.

Saturd 11. Westerly Wind. A fine Day, rather Warmer than of Late. I went out to Dine at Col Pictons. Moderate in firing till towards Evening, and then as Usual We began to be very Brisk. It is now full Moon and We can discover all their Manœuvres. We know for a certainty that We have kill'd a great many of their mules, as we See them Lay dead on the Neutral Ground, and it is not to be doubted but We have also kill'd their men.

Sund 12. Westerly Wind, fine morning. About 7 oclock a Vessel was observed coming over from the Barbary Coast. The Row Boats, Gun Boats, Xebeques, all got Under Sail. They Surrounded Her and fir'd frequently, She came close In towards our Batterys at Europa where she was exceedingly Well assisted. She fought with great Spirit and Judgment and as the Gun Boats advanc'd she fir'd Grape Shot. She was not able to Use more than 4 of her Guns for want of Hands. She has 8 Guns, 6 pounders, but had only 9 Hands including Boys. Two of his Men would not Stand to the Guns. The Enemy attempted to Board Her, but she pour'd In Grape Shott and also fir'd from Musquetoons, and by that Well Managed and Spirited Conduct was able to keep them off, and about 10 oclock We had the Good Fortune to get her safe into the New Mole. Great is the pleasure it affords every Body, who all strove to praise the Conduct of the Master before it was known what she was. It proves to be a *Polacre*, Captn McLorg Master, in the Employ of Mr Frazer in London, is 18 Days from Portsmouth, has Brought a most Wellcome Supply from England, consisting of Salt Beef, and Pork, Flour, Potatoes, Sugar, Butter, Porter, Cheese, Bacon, and Hams, &c, &c and a Number of News papers and Letters, but chiefly for the Merchants, who it is not to be doubted will avail themselves of the Necessity of the Garrison. The Master is a Resolute, Bold Irish Man. The Vessel is of 200 Ton Burthen ; a French Prize. What makes this Vessel more Welcome than Common is that it is the first We have had from England since the *Hyena* Frigate ; which was in April last. This *Polacre* brings word of a Grand Convoy that was getting ready with all Expedition for this Garrison,—and also that we are to have 15,000 Troops sent here. Soon after she got into the Mole the Wind came about strong to the East. This Morning also We got in an other Boat from Minorca, with Oil, Sugar, Cheese &c, &c. These two Welcome Vessels have afforded the Utmost Joy to every Individual. They may be realy call'd *God Sends*. This Evening We fire very much upon the Enemy. It is just a 12 Month since the Cutter call'd the *Buck*, Captn Fagg, came In ; the 2nd Sunday in Novbr.

Mond 13. Easterly Wind. The Enemy have been bringing Carriages from the Lines to the New Work, and also some people are employ'd in fixing many more pickets as if intending to throw up more Works. They have also mounted some cannon upon a Fascine Battery near the Sea Side.

Tuesd 14. Westerly Wind, fine Day. An other Boat came In from the East ; last from Alicant, brings Some Useful Articles, but We had the ill luck to Lose a Setee that was coming In from Minorca. Several of the family articles which have come in the late Boats from Minorca, and also part of what came In on Sunday from England, are Selling this Day at Auction. Suppose they will go off very high ; yet we are Bless't in having them. There is but a Small quaintity of

<table>
<tr><td>14th November, 1780.</td><td>

Potatoes; and they sold at an Astonishing price. The Govr has order'd them to be sold in Small Lots, 25 lbs each, as it is chiefly Meant to have them Sow'd, which it will be time to do in two Months. They sold at three Rials 4 quarts pr lb,—equal to fifteen pence English Money! The flour sold cheaper than any other thing, owing to there being a tolerable Quaintity in Garrison. We got a Cask, near 200 Wt, 25 Drs 4 Rs. There is a good deal of flour in the Garrison We Understand; tho' it Seems chiefly kept up for the Troops and the English.

</td></tr>
</table>

Wed 15. Westerly Wind, fine Day. The Enemy still Busy, and are forming their Boyaus of approach. It appears as if this Work was Undoubtedly intended for a Mortar Battery. It is said They have already brought some Mortars to it, but that is very Uncertain; tho' it serves to make people seem *Knowing.*

Thursd 16. Westerly Wind. Fine Cold Day. We bought a great many family Articles from the English Vessel, but all at an advanc'd and high price...as follows :—1 Teirce of Beef 85 Drs, £12 ; 1 Cask of Pork 68 Drs, £10 ; a Side of Bacon 43 Drs, £5 16s 6d ; Tongues, at pr lb 1 Dr, £0 3s 6d ; Hams at pr lb 6 Rials, £0 2s 6d ; Butter at pr lb 5 Rials, £0 2s od ; Sugar 6 Rials, £0 2s 6d ; Cheese 6 Rials, £0 2s 6d ; 100 Wt of Potatoes 45 Drs, £7 os od.

The Porter is 60 Dollars a Hogshead. N.B. It is impossible to avoid taking some part of these high pric'd articles. A Fore Qr of Mutton from Genl Boyd. This evening about 9 oclock 7 Gun Boats came over from Algezira and the Rivers, and fir'd at many parts of the Garrison, as well as upon our Ships. We return'd their fire from the Bastions &c. One of their shot came on Shore upon Mr Raleighs the Secry House, and drove In the Corner Stone, and Broke into a Room. It did no Material Harm but greatly alarm'd all the family. A very heavy fire was keep up until We drove them' off. The Batterys also keep up a Smartt fire ; but it is Supposed the Enemy are very Busy at their New Work and it is likely have sent those Boats in order to amuse the attention of the Garrison, whilst they go on, but the Captain upon the Mountain fir'd a great deal the whole time. One of the Shott from the Gun Boat hurt the Main Mast of the *Enterprize*, and the Splinters Wounded 5 Men. Also a Shot went over the Navy Hospital.

Fry 17. Westerly Wind. It is now observed that the Enemy have done a good deal of Work and are determined to go on ; in the Mean time we Fire in the most Violent Way at Some Times, particularly every Night, as it is now Dark Nights, and we know they always make use of those times. They are also at a Strong Work at Caberita point ; and have taken large Mortars from the Camp there.

Saturd 18. Westerly Wind, very Cold Day. The Enemy have added greatly this last Nt to their New Work in a continuation of their Line. The Governor has given the Work the Name of The

Mill Battery, it being near to an old Mill. I shall therefore call it by that Name. This Battery is about 1,000 yards from our Grand Battery. It appears as if they meant to add more to their Line ; and it is the opinion of the Chief Engineer that if they add two more Lines in a Certain Direction it will then be Evident they mean to attack Us. Captn Loyd upon the Batterys to Day and he fir'd Several Shott and one thirteen Inch Mortar which fell directly into the very Middle of the Work,—it threw them into a good deal of Confusion. This forenoon the Bed of the 13 Inch Mortar Split into a thousand pieces ; and in Consequence the Shell fell very Short. It got no further than the Gardens and burst amongst some of the Towns people who were out in those Gardens, but did not do any hurt. About half past Eight this Evening the Gun Boats came again. It obliged us to Fire upon them as Usual. In so doing a very Unfortunate Accident happen'd. A 32 pounder on the Kings Bastion Burst as it was going off,— Kill'd one Artillery Man upon the Spot— exactly took Him through the Middle of his Body, and separated his Head from his Body,—it greatly Wounded an other Gunner and Burnt a Man of the 12th Regt and Slightly Wounded Several Men who happen'd to be upon the Bastion. It was attended by many Uncommon Circumstances, amongst which was that of a very large piece of the Gun being thrown as far as a Quarter opposite the Bomb House, where Capt Phipps of the Engineers lives, and which is about Ninety Yards from the part where the Gun was mounted—this piece weighd 270 Wt.* It carried away a Water Spout and brought down a great deal of the Stones and Mortar belonging to the next Quarter. It fell into a little Sort of Garden and Sunk very deep into the Ground. It alarm'd the family greatly but did not do any hurt except Unpaving the Court Yard &c. The apron of the Gun was Blown into the Main Street, and many other pieces were found in different parts of the Town. It Broke away all the Banquet on that part of the Bastion went down to the Casemates under them. This accident has alarm'd and affected every Body. It was an exceeding bad Gun—and like too many others here—as the Remaining part was try'd with a Screw Borer the next Day.

Sund 19. Westerly Wind ; Cold Raw Day, and every Body Seems affected by what pass'd last Night. I went out in the forenoon but was very ill and continued so all Day. All quiet from the Enemy. They carried over a Vessel that was Supposed to be such an other as that which lately arrived from England.

Mond 20. Westerly Wind and Some Rain. The Enemy very busy all last Night, and We as Usual firing.

Tuesd 21. Westerly Wind, fine Day. The Work at Caberita point going on and at the Mill Battery. The Colonel had the Whist Party at our House in the Evening.

* *i.e.* 2 cwt. 70 lbs.

85

22nd November, 1780.

Wed 22. Westerly Wind. All the Same. Nothing very particular. I went to Sup at Lt Col Trigges this Evening. Am still exceeding Lame, and affected by the Cold Weather, and other Uncomfortable Matters. A great deal of Firing this Evening and all Night.

Thursd 23. Westerly Wind. The Enemy more advanc'd and our firing more frequent, both by Day and Nt. The family articles which came in the *Polacre* are now Selling at Auction. We gave forty five Dollars for a 100 Wt of Potatoes for Sowing at the Mount,—equal to £7 sterling.

Fry 24. Westerly Wind, exceedingly Cold. The Enemy have added greatly to their Works and are exceedingly Bold and Daring, firing upon our Towns People, and indeed every where with Small Arms. They have been employ'd for Several Days past in Collecting a very considerable quaintity of Chandaliers, Casks, Fascines and Sand Bags ; making a Depositt in the Round Tower near their Battery, and this Morning it was observed their making their Line of approach as during the foregoing Night, the Enemy have Debouched through the Lines with a Boyau of approach running from the Saillant Angle of the Well Battery, about South West, 100 feet in length. A New Method of firing was try'd from the *Montague* whilst the Govr was there about 8 oclock this Evening, at which time the Gun Boats came again and fir'd very much at the Shiping. We did not fire from the Garrison but encreased our firing from the heights. The whole Night We keep throwing Shells and Shott. Those Boats are Resolved to trouble us, —and they Effectually do So.

Saturd 25. Westerly Wind. The Colonel up upon the Mountain for Many hours this Day as well as for Several other Days, and the Govr at our House this and every Day now. I am desired to get letters ready against the Boat is expected to go which will be try'd the first Easterly Night after this. The Gun Boats came as Usual this Evening and We fir'd greatly from all parts. Several of their Shott came on Shore last Night and particularly at the Southward. Thank God, No harm as yet has happen'd from any of their Shott. This firing from these Boats is very uncertain as the Shot are often carried in a Contrary Direction.

Sund 26. Easterly Wind. Every Body Seems Busy. A Shott from a Gun Boat came last Night into the House of Mr Booth, Pratic Master. Broke thro' into the Kitchin. His House is near the Line Wall. I write to my Sister and sent it to the public packet this Day, and one to Captn Nicolls of an old Date and was meant to have gone in Septr by some Ships.

Mond 27. Westerly Wind. The Enemy greatly advanc'd in their New Work, and seem'd as if they would continue to go on ; yet we are certain that every means are try'd to hinder them by our firing. They are at too great a distance as yet to Regard it so much as we wish. They are about 200 yards too far off. The Boat not gone.

Tuesd 28. Easterly Wind, very fine Day. This Boat Still here, as the plans and papers are not ready. The Colonel and Mr Holloway exceedingly busy, putting down on the plans the progress that the Enemy make every Night, and this is attended with a good deal of attention and trouble, and keeps the Colonel in a constant State of Anxiety and Business. 28th November, 1780.

Wed 29. Easterly Wind. Dull looking Day. I write a letter to my Son and send it to Mr G. Ward. The Enemy greatly advanc'd with the New Work. About this time most of their Ships are gone to the East from Algezira, and those few that remain are Closely hauled In shore. The whole House in hurry.

Thursd 30. Easterly Wind and Raining. A *Polacre* arrived this Morning, last from Algiers, is a prize taken by Mr Andersons Vessel. She brings a Number of Useful Articles, being a French Ship, Loaded with Oil, Wine, Soap, Candles, &c, &c. It is a very fortunate Circumstance, the getting In any kind of Vessel at this Juncture. More planns getting Ready. This Boat is to go to the Eastward it being impossible to get out to the West,—and the Way of Minorca Seems the only one that is any way Safe.

Fry Decr 1. Easterly Wind. A pretty good Day. The Colonel still adding to the plans, and this Morning has afforded a good deal to put In, as the Enemy have Done a good Number of feet of Work in the course of last Night. About Noon this Day a very large Ship appear'd from the East. It was at first taken for an English Frigate, but proved to be a Ship from the Levant, Loaded with Silks and other rich Commodities for England, is a Letter of Mark, Commanded by Captain Huges, 26 Guns, 70 Men. She was Surrounded by Gun Boats and other Vessels. She came into the Harbour very Safe, and we hear is to stay only to take In Water. The Grand Parade plow'd up this Day, and Such other parts of the Town as had not been plow'd up before.

Saturd 2. Easterly Wind. Raining most of the forenoon, and appears as if there would be bad Weather. The following was in Garrison Orders this Day :—" Several officers of the Garrison having Communicated observations and hints to the Governor which have proved, and others may prove very advantageous to the Kings Service ; officers of every Rank are desired to Communicate any remarks which appear to them Useful. The Governor assures them such beneficial discoveries shall be publickly acknowledged at a proper time." About 6 oclock this Evening it began to Rain very Hard,—and Directly came on the most Violent Storm of Hail, Rain, and Thunder that I ever Remember ; which Continued about half an hour,—and happy for this Garrison it was that it lasted no longer. As it was it has done a great deal of Harm. Several old Houses thrown down, and a vast quaintity of Rubish came from the Mountain. The whole Garrison was full of Bustle and hurry. The Colonel was at the Convent* when it began and could not get away till near 9 oclock, for tho' the Violence of the Storm was only of a Short Duration, yet it continued to pour with Rain till near 11. We had continually the different Engineers coming about Drains &c. The Rain and Thunder seem'd much abatted and We were all quiet when going to Bed. The Captain upon the Mountain fir'd frequently during the Storm and all Night, as did also the officers from Prince of Oranges and Montague Bastions. It seem'd to be tolerable calm Weather when we went to Bed at 12.

Sund 3. Easterly Wind. At 6 oclock this Morning it began to Rain and Blow very Violently and Many people were fearful that it was going to be as bad as last Night. However it clear'd up. It was Showery all the Morning. The Colonel most amazingly hurried, in order to send off some papers and Despatches by the Letter of Mark which We find intends going this Night. We hear of a good deal of harm done in the New Made Gardens upon the Mountain, and at all the Grounds at the Southward. All pretty well at Mount Pleasant except that the Hail has destroy'd the Beans and Peas and the Young Salleting.† The Enemy seems rather at a Stand just now. It is supposed they are Waiting for a Supply of Fascines and Wool Bags &c, this late Wet Weather having hinder'd them a good deal. The Vessel that came In last fryday intends going away as this Evening, and in consequence the Col is exceedingly hurried in geting away his dispatches. I cannot as yet learn if it is expected that the letters which are now waiting in the post office are to be sent or not as every thing of this kind is kept a profound Secret. We have some letters at Mr Wards, which We think to send and others in the office.

Mond 4. Easterly Wind. Raining and dull Weather. The Ship did go last Night, and Captn Leslies first Lt and a Lt of Marines went Home. This Day the Colonel had a good deal of More hurry in Settling for other plans to be got Ready to go in the Boat to Minorca, which will most certainly sail the first Westerly wind. We live in a State of Earnest doubts and Expectations, which is of all Situations most distressing. The American Club Day. The Col went but came away before six oclock. It Rained all this Day and likewise at Night. We have but little Firing now. Find that the Porter which came in the last Vessel from England is already Lower'd in the price, Ten Dollars the Hogshead, and it is Supposed will be Still cheaper. We had near 500 Dollars Worth of family Articles from this Vessel.

Tuesd 5. Easterly Wind. Raining all this Day. All very quiet from Us and from the Enemy. The Whist Meeting at Lt Col Craigs. It was in Orders of the Garrison this Day :—" Lt Booth of the Corps

---

* *i.e.* Government House.
† *i.e.* Salad, see table under date December 30, 1780.

of Engineers is to have the Inspection, as Director, Under the Chief 5th December, 1780. Engineer, of all the Mines; and all Persons employ'd therein; Taking his Orders from, and reporting to, the Chief Engineer."

N.B. His appointment is Eight Shillings pr Day for the above Duty. It has given Universal Satisfaction; particularly to the Corps as Mr Booth is much Esteemed by Every Body.

Wed 6. Easterly Wind. A very Wet Morning and continued so all Day. About 9 this Evening the Captn upon the Batterys threw a Carcase at the Enemys New Work which shewed a good deal of that Battery, and He also followed it closely with Grape Shott. N.B. We have been very quiet of late from the Gun Boats.

Thursd 7. Easterly Wind. Still Raining and Wet Weather. The Enemy advancing every Night. This Evening a good deal of firing from the Montague Bastion, the Artillery officer upon that post being order'd to Fire a Certain Number every hour.*

Fry 8. Easterly Wind. Raining and bad Weather. The Enemy have added a Strong Traverss in front of the New Work and brought down some heavy Carriages, as it appears from the Deep Tracks in the Sand. Many of the *Knowing* Ones boldly pronounce there are already mortars in the Work—however the more *Steady* Persons say it is merely Conjecture. The Enemy have, and still continue to affect to shew great Matters; such as Seting out in View Mortar Sponges, Hand Spikes, &c, &c, &c, but all that is well Understood by this Garrison.

Saturd 9. Easterly Wind. A fine looking Day. In the forenoon an Experiment was try'd from Old Mole—to throw Shells from Howitzers to the Enemys New Battery. It answer'd very well for the most part. One Shell fell Directly in the front of their Work and threw down some Fascines, which they instantly repair'd. The officer who appear'd to command their party behav'd Remarkably Well, with much Seeming Coolness and Conduct, and Stood upon the Front Epaulment the whole time, and seem'd to encourage the Men. Our Captain upon the Batterys was expected to have fir'd upon the Enemy during their Working, but He did Not! The Govr Seem'd to express a surprize at his not firing. However it was amply made up by the Constant Fire He keep up all the Evening and Night, which it is not to be doubted did greatly hinder their Working. At half past Six in the Evening it began to Thunder, Rain, and Hail with the greatest Violence, much indeed as it did this Day Week. It alarm'd us a good deal, fearing it would be attended by the Same Unpleasant Consequences, but it did not continue more than about Ten Minutes,—after that it was a Settled Rain all Night.

Sund 10. Easterly Wind. Raining all Night and till about Noon.

---

* The entries for this day and the next, except as regards the weather, are transposed in the other version of the diary.

1 Decem-
1780.

A most Welcome Sight presented this Morning. A brig from Leghorn, Loaded with Wine, Brandy, and Oil, and 3 Setees from Minorca, all get Safe into the New Mole, it being impossible for the Enemys Boats to Move from over the Way. The Brig brings flying Reports with regard to an Engagement that has been between Sir George Rodney and the French in the West Indies, in which We had been Successful, and also that the fleet was gone from Cadiz ; in order it is supposed to meet the Expected fleet coming from England to this Garrison. We also hear of an Insurrection in the South America ; that it was discover by means of a Priest which We had taken. The Setees from Minorca bring as Usual, many little Useful Articles but that Governor will not let them bring Live Stock.

Mond 11. Easterly Wind. Cold and Raining. The Enemy have done a good deal last Night. The Brig brings Letters with the following accounts of the Rebellion in South America. N.B. It is just the heads of a Letter which I took.

Extract of a Letter, Dated London, Septr 26th, 80.

" The *Bellona* privateer, from Buenos Ayres, brings Word the Rebellion took place in March last, commenc'd at Aregiupa ; a general Revolt at Cochambamba, Oriero, Chicuto, and the other districts of Potosi, where the Kings Treasure is, and it had got as far down as Paraguay."

Tuesd 12. Easterly Wind. Cold and Rain. The Colonel not Well ; did not go to the Parade. An auction of the Prize Goods. The Evening was fine. The Whist Meeting at Col Kellets. Good deal of firing this Evening and also in the forenoon, at the Enemy's being in the Gardens all Day.

Wed 13. Easterly Wind. Cold Morning. The Colonel not well. It Rained hard this forenoon and continued to do so all Day. At Night it came on very Violently and brought down still more Rubish.

Thursd 14. Easterly Wind. The Colonel better and at the Parade.

Thursd 21. Westerly Wind. This forenoon a Vessel appear'd ; coming In from Under the Barbary Coast. She prov'd to be a Kings Cutter, the *Speedwell*, from Portsmouth, commanded by Lt Gibson, bringing Dispatches for the Govr, does not chuse to mention the exact time she has been from Engd, and the whole Seems to be a profound Secret. She yesterday fell In with one of the Enemies half Galleys. As the Cutter lay over near Ceuta the Enemy sent out an Arm'd Boat to see what she was, and from the manner she came In Concluded she was only a Small Vessel from Ireland, as it was formerly the Custom to send Cutters of this kind Loaded with Provisions. After the Boat had observed her a Galley came out from Ceuta and attempted to Board Her, in doing which a Spainiard fir'd a Musketoon which

greatly Wounded Lt Gibson. The Galley was drove off, having first 21st Decem-
Received a Number of Hard Knocks; and it is Suposed she was ber, 1780.
hardly able to get Into Ceuta. The Kings Cutter got Safe into the
New Mole. The Lt was the only Person hurt on Board. He was
Drawing his Sword at the time the Gun hurt him.

Fry 22. Westerly Wind. Very Wet, Cold Weather. Lt Gibson
is not Mortaly Wounded We hope, is brought on Shore to the Navy
Hospital. It is keep a profound Secret as to what this Cutter is come
out for. Therefore all Manner of Conjectures are forming. It is most
Certain that it is on business of Consequence. We also Seem to
Understand that a Frigate came out from England at this same time.
There has not been one Single letter for any Body, for not a person
on board the Cutter knew of their Destination when they were order'd
at a Moments Warning to go out to sea from Spithead, and the Lt
Received Positive Orders not to open his Instructions till he arrived
at a Certain Latitude. This is the only Kings Vessel we have had
Since the *Hyena* Frigate in April last. There is not a Man on board
allow'd to come on Shore, or to answer any Questions that are Ask'd
of Them.

Saturd 23. Easterly Wind, raining hard, at Day Break. A Snow
arriv'd this Morning from the West, a privatter from Portsmouth,
call'd the *Hannah*, Captn Venture, belonging to Mr Turnbull, She
came last from Lisbon, from which Port she brings Letters dated 5th
of Decbr. She has Various Articles for this place, such as Hams,
Bacon, Butter, Leather, &c, &c, and a Number of letters for different
Persons in the Garrison. We got Letters from our Family dated 26th
October. Our Son informs Us of the Royals* being order'd for foreign
service, and were at that time at Portsmouth, perhaps would embark
in a week. This has afforded Us a good deal of Concern, and the
More So as their destination is a total Secret. I have the happiness
of hearing that all the family were well. We still remain in Ignorance
both with respect to where that Regt was going; or if there is any
time fix'd for a Convoy's coming out to this Garrison. This Evening
the following after Garrison Orders were given out :—" There being the
Strongest reasons to believe that Colonel Ross is appointed Colonel
to the 72nd Regt or Royal Manchester Volunteers, altho' no official
Notice has yet been received by the Governor, He is therefore only
to do the Duty of Colonel in the Garrison and no longer to act Lt
Col to the 39th Regt, Untill further Orders, and there being the
strongest reasons to believe that Captains Baugh, and Mercier of the
39th Regt and Captain Hamilton of the 56th Regt are appointed
Brevet Majors they are to do Duty as such, till further Orders.

Sund 24. Westerly Wind. A Cold Morning. Various opinions
of what the Kings Cutter and this last Vessel has brought with regard

---

* His own regiment, which he afterwards commanded. See preface.

to News, particularly the Cutter. We hear that the *Brilliant* Frigate of 36 Guns is hourly expected, that she left England the Same time the Cutter did, being it is Supposed charged with Some public Despatches. Got a very large and fine hind Qr of Mutton from General Boyd, 22 lbs. This may be called a very Cool, Melancholy Season and much unlike what We us'd to have in this Garrison. We cannot make any great preparation for Christmas Day.

Mond 25. Westerly Wind. Christmass Day. A very fine Day indeed, and Usher'd In by a most truly Welcome Circumstance, viz., a *Polacre* from Liverpool, Loaded with flour, Butter, Hams, &c,—no less than 300 Casks of flour which is so much a greater Blessing as it now is openly known that there is not more than three Days flour for the Inhabitants in the Garrison. This Vessel may be plac'd amongst some of the *God Sends* that we have experienced since the Blockade, and has put every Body into high Spirits. The Boat is to sail this Night for Minorca by which I send several letters ; and a Long one to my Sister, acknowledging the Receipt of the letters which arrived on Saturday last, and had a letter inclosed to a friend of Mr Wards, for my Son. At Noon this Day the Spainish Deserter who came In from the Enemy upon Septr 29th and who has always been suspected to be a Spy was taken hold of upon Suspicion and instantly sent Prisoner to the Provost. He was Search'd and many papers found upon Him. He has been very Closely Watched of late by Captn Uniacke of 58th whose Company is quartered upon Windmill Hill. This man went it seems, into the Soldiers Barracks there ; and asked them to lend him some Sealing Wax. The Captain happen'd to be in some part of the Barrack and heard him. He directly went up to him and ask'd him what He wanted with Sealing Wax. He Directly laid hold of Him and had Him Searched. Several Suspicious papers were found upon Him, particularly a Letter, wrote in English and intended to be sent to a Colonel Nugent who has the Regt He belongs to. It acknowledges in that letter, his having Recd several sums of Money from Col Nugent and also letters. He also tells the Way that He has plan'd for his geting away. He was directly taken up to the Provost at the Moorish Castle.

Tuesd 26. Westerly Wind. A very fine day indeed. The Boat with the packet, and also an other went away last Night. I went out this forenoon and call'd upon Several and went to the South Bastion. Variety of opinions with respect to the Deserter and what will be done with Him. He has not been examined as yet. The Enemy have brought four Mortars into St Carlos Battery, as We find they have given that Name to the New Work. They are at Work this Day,—and last Night. N.B. I omitted to mention that Divine Service was performed yesterday in the inside of the Court Yard at the Convent, Round under the Colonade, and afterwards the Sacrament administer'd at the Judges Court House. This is the first time 26th December, 1780. that the Service has been at the Convent since the Church was made use of for a Store House. It is now full of Dry Provisions. Every Sunday the Service has been under the Kings Bastion, when ever the Weather allow'd.*

Wed 27. Westerly Wind. A very fine Day. The Govr and the Colonel went Round to Europa and Examin'd the Boom at New Mole. We keep up a Smart firing all this Day upon the Enemys Working Partys.

Thursd 28. Westerly Wind. Rainy. A Man of 39th Regt who was confin'd in Barrack Yard for Stealing a Watch made his Escape from the Centry who had him under his charge. It is supposed he is upon the Mountain. We go to Captn Phipps in the Evening.

Fry 29. Easterly Wind. A Spainish Setee was seen off Europa and after our firing upon Her from thence the *Enterprize* Frigate sent out Boats and brought Her In, but every Body had quited Her and taken to a Small Boat. She was going to Malaga from Algezira, had a Number of letters on board, which most likely may be useful. The Setee is a very pretty Vessel and may be Worth about £150. This Day I had a Minorca Pig kill'd; which I bought in Septr last. I gave 22 Cobbs for it. It now weighs 100 Wt beside the Inside, which as pork is now sold at Six Rials a pound would amount to 75 Dollars and she cost 33 Dollars. Sent hind Qr of this Pork to Genl Boyd weight 24 lb, and a neck to Mrs Phipps.

Saturd 30. Easterly Wind. Cold Raw Day. No Comfortable preparation for the New Year. Altho the Garrison is Well Supplied with Variety of every thing except Live Stock, yet is every family Article so extravagantly Dear, that the poor sort are Dreadfully off. Three Guineas has been ask'd for a Roasting Pig, and the cheapest are sold for two. On board the Liverpool Vessel is almost every useful thing,—Corn'd Rounds of Beef, pickeld Tripe, Herrings, Bacon, Hams, and a vast Number of other articles, all to be Sold at public auction. The Rounds of Beef Sold for Seven Rials pr pound, which is equal to three shillings, and they are very Large for the most of them; a Round that was bought by Colonel Ross, 35 Dollars. I shall endeavour to set down the prices of family Necessaries at the Close of this year, and compare them with what those Necessaries were last year. It must be Remark'd that as We have been So Lucky as to get In three Vessels lately from England it has lower'd the high price of some few articles. At this time last year there was a few Oxen and Cows kill'd but that is not the case now. We have not had any Beef for many Weeks past. The last sold for 7 Rials. There has not been any Mutton for Months at the Market, nor any Goat of late.

---

* The other version of the diary says " upon the Kings Bastion."

h Decem-
, 1780.

Fish has been at an astonishing price all this last year, particularly Hake Fish. We give a Cobb for what used to be only 2 Rials. Vegetables are now pretty reasonable, owing to the Number of Gardens at the Southward, and every Person is obliged to send to the public market all they do not want in their own family. A Large good Cabbage is sold for two Rials and a half (equal to a Shilling.) Upon the whole we may think ourselves very fortunately Supplied; our greatest Wants are Firing, and Wine for the Troops. The Large Supply that came some weeks agoe of Lemons has been of the Utmost Benefit to the Troops. The Scurvy is greatly abatted. The few Coals that were left on board some of the Ships which have been here many months have been sold lately. Sixteen pounds sterling pr Chauldron. Soap is cheaper than it was.

	1779.			1780.					
	D.	R.	Q.	D.	R.	Q.	£	s.	d.
Beef pr lb	0	4	0	.	.	.	0	1	9
Veal do	1	0	0	1	2	0	0	3	8
Pork do	0	6	0	0	6	0	0	2	4
Goat do	0	6	0	.	.	.	0	2	4
Turkey a piece	18	0	0	.	.	.	2	18	6
Fowls do	2	0	0	3	0	0	0	10	4
Geese do	9	0	0	6	6	0	1	1	0
Ducks do	3	0	0	3	0	0	0	10	4
Roasting Pig ...	.	.	.	13	4	0	2	2	0
Pigeons, a pair	1	4	0	2	0	0	0	7	0
Sausages, lb	.	.	.	1	1	0	0	3	10
Flour pr lb ...	0	2	0	0	1	0	0	0	4
Peas do	0	1	0	0	0	8	0	0	2
Butter do	0	6	0	0	4	0	0	1	4
Cheese do	1	0	0	0	2	8	0	1	0
Sugar do	1	0	0	0	4	8	0	1	6
Hams do	.	.	.	0	4	0	0	1	4
Candles do	0	6	0	0	2	8	0	1	0
Eggs a piece ...	0	0	8	0	1	0	0	0	4
Sallad oil pint (spelt Sallet in the other copy)	0	4	8	0	3	0	0	1	2
Good tea pr lb	6	0	0	5	0	0	1	4	2
Soap pr lb	0	4	0	0	2	0	0	0	8

Soap has been exceedingly Dear all this last year at pr lb 4 Rials but of late is 2 Rials.

(To be continued).

A LADY'S EXPERIENCES IN THE GREAT SIEGE OF GIBRALTAR (*1779-83*).

BEING THE DIARY FROM 1ST JUNE, 1779, TO 13TH JUNE, 1781, OF MRS. GREEN, THE WIFE OF LIEUT.-COLONEL GREEN, CHIEF ENGINEER OF GIBRALTAR (AFTERWARDS LIEUT.-GENERAL SIR WILLIAM GREEN, BART., CHIEF ENGINEER OF GREAT BRITAIN, 1786—1802). EDITED BY COLONEL E. R. KENYON, R.E.

(Concluded).

JANUARY THE FIRST 1781.

Monday. Easterly Wind. No sort of Notice taken of this Day upon the Parade—or in any other respect—by the Governor. It was a Cold, Unpleasant Morning, and continued an Uncomfortable Day in all Respects. We had a party at dinner but by no means either cheerful or Easy, as might have been wish'd. The Enemy are not busy to Day. This Day Some Spainish Letters and papers which were found on board the Setee which our Men of Wars Boats brought in on last fryday were brought to the Governor, to our House. I saw several but they gave no very Material account,—mostly seem'd private family Letters; except a Couple which were wrote it should appear by good Judges of our, as well as of their own New Works; but those letters were not Sign'd. There were also some Beads and a Crucifix and other articles belonging to a Priest who had been too much hurried in geting away. There is likewise Some Caps and a few things belonging to a Lady as we suppose, but that is only Conjecture as every Person had quited the Setee, nor was there any Live Creature left but one Pig. These things are all in Captn Leslie's posession. He talks of sending back the Lady's Caps &c and the Letters except those two above mention'd, but I do think the Govr will hardly Yield to Him. It would be highly improper to send any Letters back; that would hurt the People who wrote them.

Tuesd 2. Easterly Wind. A much finer Day than yesterday. A Man of the 72nd Regt Deserted last Night from Bay Side Guard. The Man of the 39th has not been heard of. It is supposed He has either got clear off or has met with the fate of some others who have Dash'd to pieces in trying to get off. Very little firing from Us upon the Enemy. The Col at Captn Loyds whist Party this Evening.

Wed 3. Easterly wind and very Cold Raw Day. An experiment was try'd today, viz., a New Invention for proving, or rather trying of Cannon, upon the Kings Bastion, Under the Direction of Lt Fredrick

3rd January,
1781.

of the 72nd (Son to Sir Charles Fredrick, Surveyor Genl of the Office of Ordnance). It gave much Satisfaction to every Body ; the Govr also seem'd Well pleased ! ! !

Thursd 4. Easterly Wind. A Cold Raw Day. All quiet from the Enemy. Find myself exceedingly indisposed, but being under an Engagement to Sup out I was obliged to keep up as much as possible ; and in Consequence I went out to Mrs Fancourts. Very little firing. Auctions every Day. Some times the Several Articles Sold pretty well. The English Rounds of Beef are very good ; but are got up to an amazing price, viz., 7 Rials pr lb equal to 3 shillings.

Fry 5. Easterly Wind. Clear Cold Day. Colonel Ross gives a Dinner to the whole of the officers of the 72nd Regt, Supposing himself the Colonel of that Regt.* It consisted of a very Large Number, 43. All Ended with great Harmony, they sat late. Many People Wonder that the Colonel should take a step of this kind till He was quite Confirm'd in his having got the Regt. He is now in very high spirits and seems to have forgot all past Circumstances. We do not Fire now but little, except when any thing in particular is doing.

Saturd 6. Easterly Wind, fine Day. Moving powder from the South into the Town Magazines and the Castle. The Enemy have been throwing up a great deal of Sand and carrying on their Boyau toward Fort Barbara. This Even the following was in Garrison after Orders :—"The Morning Divine Service to be in the Convent Court to Morrow and on the first Sunday of every following Month."

Sund 7. Easterly Wind. Cold Day. Col up very Early to go to the Southward with the Govr. Things not very agreable, either publickly or privately. Col Din'd out at Col Craigs.

Mond 8. Easterly Wind ; Cold and Unpleasant. A most Uncomfortable Day, and Much discontent in Garrison. The American club Day.

Tuesd 9. Easterly Wind, fine Day. Am taking very ill, with pains in my Limbs and in great. Uneasiness in all Respects. The whist Meeting at Captn Hastings.

Wed 10. Easterly Wind and Raining Hard. This, and every Morning of late, We have been trying Experiments by firing from the Old Mole towards the New Work, sometimes with good Success. I am exceedingly ill at this time. Colonel also indisposed. Mr Booth taken ill.

Thursd 11. Easterly Wind. Early this Morning two Moorish Vessels that have been at the Orange Grove for more than 12 Days and which We could not tell what to make of, came to the Mole under protection of a Flagg of Truce, and were received by a Flagg of Truce from Us. They are come from Barbary and bring over all the Christians that were sent from this Garrison some Months agoe, by

* See December 23rd, 1780.

order of the Emperor, beginning with the English Consul and Mr ^{11th January,} Butlers family &c &c. The Emperor would not allow any of Them ^{1781.} or the English Consul to remain in any Part of Barbary. Mr Butler the Dutch Consul who left this Garrison 16 Months agoe is also come away. They were not allowed to bring any thing with them except their Cloaths, and had only 5 hours Notice.

Fry 12. Easterly Wind. Very Severe Cold Weather, and find myself greatly indisposed. The Colonel much distress'd about Mr Booth, and other very Uncomfortable Circumstances. Do not hear that the People from Barbary bring over any News. Some Coals which came in the late Vessels from England are sold upon the Parade for a Hundred Dollars a Chaldron. They are bought by Government.

Saturd 13. Easterly Wind. Raw Cold Day. I have not been down stairs since Tuesday last, nor do I think I shall for some time to come. The Colonel also much indisposed. It is Still Reported that the Enemy have got Mortars into the New Battery. N.B. By a Spainish Gazette which the Consul got whilst the Vessels lay at the Orange Grove We find the Enemy have given the Name of St. Carlos to the New Battery, it is Supposed in Honor of their King.

This Day the Regulations for Officers Provisions from the 15th Janry to the 11th Febry 1781.

Officers pr Month. 28 lb of Bread ; 4 lb of Beef; 4 Do of Pork ; 10 oz of Butter ; 1½ lb of Cheese (in lieu of 2 lb of Beef) ; 4 pints of Kidney Beans, or Carravances ; 4 pints of Wheat ; 3 lb of Flour ; 2 lb of Raisons.

The Wheat, Kidney Beans, Raisons, and Flour are in lieu of 12 pints of Pease and 30 oz of Butter.

4 lb of Beef and 12 pints of Oatmeal to be paid for.

Men pr Week. 7 lb of Bread ; 1 lb of Beef; 1 lb of Pork ; 1 pint of peas ; 2½ oz of Butter ; 6 oz of cheese (in lieu of ½ lb of Beef) ; ¾ lb of Flour, 1 pint of Wheat, 1 Do of Kidney beans, ½ lb of Raisons (in lieu of 3 pints of peas and 7 oz of Butter) ; ¼ pint of Vinegar, 1 lb of Beef, 3 pints of Oatmeal (to be paid for).

Sund 14. Westerly Wind. It began to Rain at Day break and continued to do so till 11. It then clear'd up a little, but about 6 in the Evening came on a very Violent Storm of Thunder and Lightning, attended with a Torrent of Rain. It continued till 12 at Night and brought down as Usual a large quaintity of Stone and Rubish from the Mountain ; then abatted and afterwards came on but with less Violence. The Colonel was at Home some part of the time.

Mond 15. Westerly Wind. Raining at Guard Mounting. A Frigate belonging to the Enemy was drove from Algezira during the Storm last Night, and was carried up to the two Rivers. Their Camp and New Batterys, all Seem under Water. We do not keep up much firing now. This afternoon a Mortar was Fir'd from Montague Bastion to St Carlos upon a New plan of the Govrs. It was sunk

15th January, 1781. down in the Ground. It Seem'd to answer tolerably Well. N.B. 4 Inches of Rain fell last Night.

Tuesd 16. Westerly Wind. Raining very hard at Guard Mounting and continued so all the forenoon. The Colonel had the Whist party at his House. I was confin'd by great Indisposition to my Bed Room. I have been ill with this complaint, a Violent sickness, and a Rash all over me for two months past, but it is now Worse.

Wed 17. Westerly wind. Blowing Hard. Find myself Uncommonly ill, all this Day. The Enemy very quiet. A very Dark Night,—exceedingly Cold and Uncomfortable.

Thursd 18. Westerly Wind. In the Course of last Night a Cutter Privatteer, the *Tartar*, Captn Gibson came In. She is only 14 Days from Ports, is come with Dispatches to the Govr and to Captain Leslie, brings some Useful Articles for this Garrison. We learn that the King has declar'd War with the Dutch, and also that our Fleet had Return'd to Ports after having had Sight of the French Fleet. A great deal of News seems to be flying about.

Fryd 19. Westerly Wind. A better looking Morning than We have had of Late. There has been a Promotion of Majors by Brevet, We hear, and also that Genl Skinner Died on Christmass Day.* We have not got any letters by this last Cutter ; the Articles which are to be Sold are belonging to Mr. Turnbull. We get a Round of Beef, 42 lb, as yet we do not know the price. N.B. Find it is to be $4\frac{1}{2}$ Rials pr lb.

Saturd 20. Westerly Wind, fine looking Day. The Col went up to breakfast at the Rock Guard, came down in the forenoon very much indisposed, and continued ill all the Rest of the Day. He has been very indifferent Some Weeks, but has not Chused to confine himself.

Sund 21. Westerly Wind. The Colonel taken very ill, sent for Baynes. He continued in his Room all Day, and for the most part very ill indeed.

Mond 22. Westerly Wind. Colonel no better ; still in his Room ; takes Physic this Day, and does not see any Body. Very ill myself. Get $14\frac{1}{2}$ lbs of English Mutton, 10 Rials pr pound.

Tuesd 23. Westerly Wind, fine Weather. The Colonel still in the same way, keeps his Room. Two of the Privatters, Captn Venture and McLorge, saild to the Eastward last Night, but I had not any letters on board. Whist Meeting at Judge Frazers.

Wed 24. Westerly Wind. Fine in the forenoon. The Colonel a little better ; gets out into the Dressing Room ; but grew much

---

* He was then 81 years of age and still Chief Engineer of Great Britain, which office he had held for 23 years. His recommendations on Green's reports on the fortifications of Gibraltar are in the British Museum : Add MSS. 10034. He was succeeded by Colonel James Bramham.

Worse at 3 oclock, and continued very ill all the afternoon ; his Dis- 24th January, order Seems mostly upon his Nerves ; attended with flying pains in 1781. Head and Breast.

Thursd 25. Westerly Wind ; the Colonel very indifferent, takes a Medicine Early in Morning, which affects Him. He continued greatly indisposed all Day. Miss Evelegh Died last Night, after having been long indisposed ; tho' not confin'd to the House above 12 Days. She was near 13 years old, was buried at Night, very privately, at South port.

Fry 26. Westerly wind, a fine looking Day. The Col has had a very bad Night, but grew Easier about Noon, and Walk'd into the Garden a little. A Man of Hardenburghs Deserted last Night. N.B. A Serjant of the 56th Deserted from Landport Guard last Sunday Morning ; He has left a Wife and children behind. He was in Debt.

Saturd 27. Easterly Wind. The Colonel has had a pretty good Night ; is better to Day but Seems low and Weak. 2 more men of Hardenburghs Deserted last Night. This makes four this week.

Sund 28. Easterly Wind. The Colonel very poorly this Morning and continued so all forenoon. A Vessel arrived from Leghorn this Day, belonging to Mr. Anderson, Loaded with Wines and Brandy &c, says that in Her passage here she saw a Man of Wars Long Boat with three Men's Jackets and some oars. It was the Boat belonging to the *Brilliant* Frigate. He could not get Her, as He was chased by two Xebeques. About Noon the Col grew exceedingly ill ; and We were obliged to send to Doctor Baynes who Bled Him, and He Seem'd rather Easier for it.

Mond 29. Easterly Wind ; the Col much better, and continued so till Evening, had then a little attack of His complaint, which indeed Seems mostly upon his Spirits. Two of Hardenburghs Deserted.

Tuesd 30. Easterly Wind. Very Dull Raw Day. The Colonel but very indifferent, and the Weather not good enough to allow Him to go out. 2 Setees arrived from Minorca in 20 Days, bring Word that the *Brilliant* was there when they came away, but is coming Down Here. These Vessels bring a few Supplies. The Col was better this Evening. Whist Meeting at Col Craigs.

Wed 31. Easterly Wind, better Day. The Colonel finds himself Low and rather Weak, but as the Weather was soft He went out on Horseback about half past 11, Mr Holloway with Him. It is just 11 Days since He was down stairs. He return'd before 2, and Seem'd tolerably well in Evening.

The whole of this Month has passed with very little Firing upon the Enemy, but a Number of Shott and Shells have been fir'd by Way of Experiments from the old Mole and other parts, some with tolerable Success, others very bad. The Enemy also have been trying many Experiments, and have got Mortars in Boats, and likewise

<table>
<tr><td style="vertical-align:top; width:20%">31st January, 1781.</td><td>they fire shells from the Camp, Seemingly to know the Ranges, &c., but none pointed to the Garrison. They have an astonishing Number of Fascines and Traverses at St Carlos. During this Month We have had a good deal of Rain. We have very fortunately had a happy Number of Useful Articles brought by the Several Vessels, and the Garrison is well Supplied in some articles. The greatest Want now is of Firing and Fresh Stock. The flour also will be growing Short for the Inhabitants, and also Corn for the Poultry, and what few Cows and Sheep which are now remaining.</td></tr>
</table>

Thursd February 1. Easterly Wind. Colonel rather better. It was fine Weather at 12, when He Rode out to the Southward. In the afternoon He grew indisposed and was very poorly all Evening, and worse when going to Bed. A Man of the 56th in attempting to Desert fell down the Rock and was Dash'd to pieces. A Party of Miners who was Working not far from there, took him up. They likewise found the Body of a Serjant of the 73rd Regt who deserted about two Months agoe, and He had Shar'd the Same Fate. There is a Man of the 56th who was Concerned in the Same Scheme as the Man who has Suffer'd, and has turn'd Kings Evidence. He was to have gone off with the other Man and Some More ; but was Disguised in Liquor and dropt Some hints, which occasion'd him to be taken into confinement, where He made a Confession of all He knew.

Fry 2. Easterly Wind. The Colonel has had a very bad Night ; and could not get up to Breakfast. Seem'd very ill all the forenoon. The Govr here this Morning. A very Cold Windy Day. He walk'd out for half an Hour, but seems much worse than yesterday. Mr. Pierson Died this Night, aged 86.

Saturd 3. Easterly Wind. The Colonel rather better, did not go to Parade ; or ride out to Day, continued pretty Well all the Evening.

Sund 4. Easterly Wind. The Colonel had a good Night, but as the Day turn'd out very indifferent He did not go out at all. Cold Raw Weather.

Mond 5. Easterly Wind, fine soft Morning. The Colonel tolerable Well, but did not go to the Morning Parade, and was very indifferent in the Evening. He did not go to the American Club.

Tuesd 6. Easterly Wind. The Colonel at the Parade ; went to Whist Party at Col Kellets.

Wed 7. Easterly Wind. Col at Grand Parade, seem'd much indisposed all Day. Grew a little Better in the Evening, and when going to Bed.

Thursd 8. Easterly Wind. This Morning a Deserter came In from the New Battery, a Catalan. He reports that We have kill'd a great many People and a Captn of Horse. He says there are 8 Mortars keep Loaded in St Carlos Battery, to fire upon the Ships no doubt. He also says that the Serjant of the 56th who Deserted on 21st Jan hung himself in the Camp the Night He got there.

Captn Martin upon the Batterys this Day and Fired very much all 8th February, the Evening, and the whole Night long. 1781.

Fry 9. Easterly Wind. This Morning a Privatter Cutter arrived from Minorca in 14 days. She brings Word that the *Brilliant* Frigate is cruizing about. This Cutter is to go to Engd in a Day or two. This Evening the Colonel was not very well. I was also very ill.

Saturd 10. Easterly Wind; fine Day. Colonel at Parade, very indifferent in forenoon, better when going to Bed.

Sund 11. Easterly Wind. Cold Raw Day; Colonel rather better; and everything pretty Easy. I write a long Letter to my Sister and sent it to the office. All Well in Evening. A Man of 72nd Regt Deserted.

The Provisions from the 12th Febry to the 11th of March 1781.

Officer pr Month. Bread as usual; 4 lb of Beef; 4 lb of Pork; 10 oz of Butter; 1 pint of Oil; 1½ lb of cheese; 4 pints of Peas; 4 pints of Kidney Beans; 4 pints of Wheat; 1½ Do of Rice; 1½ lb of Raisons; 4 lb of Beef, 12 pints of Oatmeal (to be paid for).

Men pr Week. Bread as usual; 1 lb of Beef; 1 lb of Pork; 2½ oz of Butter; ¼ pint of Oil; 1 Do of Peas; 6 oz of Cheese; 1 pint of Kidney Beans; 1 Do of Wheat; 6 oz of Rice; 6 oz of Raisons; 1 lb of Beef (to be paid for).

N.B. Soft Bread the first Week. Buisquit afterwards till further Orders.

Mond 12. Easterly Wind. Colonel rather better. All tolerable in Evening. The Cutter did not go as was expected last Night.

Tuesd 13. Westerly Wind. I write an other letter to my Sister, which I mean to send by Mr Logie. The Colonel better, and went to Major Vinogles. The Whist Meeting.

Wed 14. Westerly Wind. Col pretty Well and continued so; fine Day.

Thursd 15. Westerly Wind. Colonel at Parade, but finds his Eyes painful. He was very indifferent in the Evening. N.B. Two of the Oxen belonging to the Kings Works were sold yesterday, the Colonel not being able to keep them all lest the Grain and Provision for the Cattle would not hold out. He got 100 Guineas for them; one was Killed for the Market this Day, very good Meat; and Sold at a Dollar per lb.

Fry 16. Easterly Wind, an exceeding fine Day. The Colonels Eyes better, but finds an Uneasy pain in his Mouth. It seems to be a Rheumatick pain. We had a Large Company at dinner this Day, Davies family, Col Ross, &c, &c, and we Dress't our English Round of Beef. It weighed 42 lb, and turned out exceedingly good.

17th February, 1781.

Saturd 17. Easterly Wind; the Colonel very much indisposed with his Mouth and Head. The Cutter not gone. A Cold Raw Day. Col ill at Night.

Sund 18. Easterly Wind. The Cutter gone last Nt. Much talk of the Memorial Relating to the Regts,* Most of which are gone home. Colonel very poorly in Evening.

Mond 19*th*. Easterly Wind. Colonel very much indisposed all Day. At Noon a *Polacre* came from Minorca in 5 Days, brings some letters and a few Supplies. This Evening all was very much Distress'd and Indisposed.

Tuesd 20. Westerly Wind. Cold Day but very clear and good Weather. The Colonel much indisposed but in pretty Easy Spirits.

Mem^m in Garrison Orderly Book.

" After each Regt is Reviewed they will march from the Sands and occupy the following Posts :—

12th Regt...Montague Bastion to South End of the Saluting Battery.

39th Regt...Ragged Staff, the fleche, and to South Shed.

56th Regt...Prince of Hesses Battery ; Grand Battery, and to Montague Bastion.

58th Regt...From South Shed, the New Mole, and Rossia.

72nd Regt...Four Companys quartered at the bottom of Irish Town, to pass thro' the Sally Port, Navy Yard, and occupy the whole Cover'd Way of Water port. Six Companys Kings Bastion and to Church Battery.

73rd Regt...From Rossia to Dead Mans Hole and to send a Party to occupy Europa Gate.

The Commanding officers to Report to the Governor the Day before the Review the Manner in which they are to March from the Ground to their Posts.

56th and Hardenburghs not to Fire but to go thro' the Motions. The other Regts to Fire the Parapet firing."

Wed 21. Westerly Wind, very Cold indeed. The Colonel rather better. This Morning an other Vessel arrived from Minorca, brings a very good Supply of Wine, Oil, Sugar, and some Wood for Fires. Had a Fore Qr of Mutton from Genl Boyd.

Thursd 22. Westerly Wind, exceeding Cold. Colonel but indifferent, better in Evening.

Fry 23. Westerly Wind. Still indisposed, could not go out.

Saturd 24. Westerly Wind, still very cold. The Colonel rather better.

Sund 25. Westerly Wind. The Colonel better. Very cold Weather.

* This was a respectful memorial to the Governor drawing attention to the inadequacy of the officers' pay owing to the high rate of exchange and the great cost of all necessaries, and also to their non-participation in the recent extensive army promotions.—Drinkwater, pp. 140-1.

Mond 26. Westerly Wind. The Colonel a good deal better. The 12th Regt reviewed. All Well. 26th February, 1781.

Tuesd 27. Westerly Wind. Colonel Better ; 39th Reviewed. All quiet with that Regt. The Colonel went out after Breakfast to the Guard Mounting, and Seem'd pretty well when He return'd. We had Captn Phipps family to Eat some of the Mutton ; and Mrs Fancourt in Evening. Mrs Rogers Married this Evening to Lt Wilks of Artillery. Col Ross has made up a New Uniform, the Lappels of the 72nd Colour, but no No on the Buttons.

Wed 28. Westerly Wind, fine Morning. The Colonel not at the 56th Review, but went out afterwards to Guard Mounting. All pretty Well.

During the Course of this Month the Enemy have been very quiet. They are not often at Work at St Carlos. They realy seem as if they intended to remain as they are ; Unless Urg'd on by any New Manœuvres of ours. One thing they certainly do, which is to be very Mindful of Signals ; and other attentions upon their Coast. We can not help observing that We have Undoubtedly highly Mortified Don Barcelo ; as it is Evident He can not keep so good a Look out as He did at first ; or else We should not have got In so many little Vessels, &c &c from the East, all of which have been of the Utmost Service to this Garrison. Could We only get a Flour Ship and some Coals our greatest Wants would then be amply Supplied.

During the whole of this Month I have been a good deal indis-posed, and keep Low, by a Constant Complaint that has attended me for the last 4 Weeks, which makes me keep still in the House, and some times greatly affects my Spirits. I have been Under the Necessity of keeping up, tho' with some difficulty, as the Colonel has been much indisposed, and it has been the Utmost desire and atten-tion of my whole Mind to pay every possible Regard to his Health ; the More So as his Complaints always fall upon his Nerves, and occasions many Unpleasing Consequences.

Thursd March the first. Westerly Wind. Fine Day. Colonel did not go to the 58th Review.

Fry 2. Westerly Wind. Very clear Day, but Cold. Colonel did not go to the Field to see the 72nd but met them as they return'd to their Alarm Posts. They made it very late ; having so much to do. The Colonel not well. Colonel Ross did not Join the Regt but was in the New Uniform. He dined with the Corps at the Govrs.

Saturday 3. Easterly Wind. Blowing exceedingly hard. The Colonel went out to the Southward ; to see the 73rd take their Posts. They had two pieces of Cannon in the Field, and made a very good Review. The Col at Mr Holloways in Evening.

Sund 4. Easterly Wind. Blowing exceedingly hard all Night. The Colonel went to Guard Mounting this Morning. A Brig taken over to Algezira this Day : She had English Colours ; came from the East ; had 20 Guns.

Mond 5. Easterly Wind, fine Day. Colonel rather better ; did not go to Hardenburgs Review, but to their Alarm Posts. It was a very Warm pleasant Day.

Tuesd 6. Easterly Wind. Cold Day. Redans Review. The Colonel as Usual, at Alarm Posts. A Flagg of Truce this Day from the Enemy, Relating to Major Freake, &c. Colonel at Captn Hastings this Evening. The Whist Meeting.

Wed 7. Easterly, Cold Raw Day. De la Mottes Review. Colonel as Usual. Just as the Regt had got to their Alarm Posts ; viz., the Kings Bastion, a Man went off from Landport where He was on Guard. A Serjant observed Him Walking towards the Barrier Gates ; and call'd to Him, but He at once set off, and altho' the Guard instantly Fired, as they did from the Lines and upon the Mountain, with Ball and Grape Shott, yet He escaped and got into Fort Carlos. There were more than 500 Musket Balls fired. He was one of the 72nd Regt.

Thursd 8. Easterly Wind. Cold and Raw. Colonel rather better, goes to Guard Mounting now, seems Low at Times, has got his appetite Well.

Fry 9. Easterly Wind. Same Weather. The Colonel better. Auctions every Day. Chiefly Prize and Ship Goods.

Saturd 10. Easterly Wind. Dry Cool Weather. We had a Heifer kill'd. It weighed 200 Wt. We did not sell any but parted it amongst our Friends, keeping what parts We chose. It turns out very pretty Looking Meat. It is about a Year and Eight Months old. A Sir Loin to Genl Boyd.

Mond 12. Easterly Wind. Looks Dull like Rain. The Govr much displeased this Morning, owing to the Neglect of the Two Captains upon Picquet last Night, one of which totaly forgot to go His Rounds during the Course of the Night. The other only Went half the Rounds. It is supposed some Serious Orders or Consequences will follow such a great Neglect of Duty. It occasions much Talk. One of those Captns was Captn Pigot 56th, the other a Hanoverian captain.

Tuesd 13. Easterly Wind. Still like Rain. This Days Orders were as follows :—"The Captains of the Picquet Rounds are in future to report to the field officer of the Day the hour they went their Rounds and the Commanders of all Guards are to mention in their Reports the hours they were Visited and What Rounds." The Whist Meeting at our House this Evening. We understand that some very particular orders are to be made known as to Morrow.

Wed 14. Easterly Wind ; a little Rain this Morning. At Noon all Commanding officers were employ'd in reading a very Severe Note from the Governor in consequence of the late very great Neglect of

Duty in the two Captns upon the Picquet,—also a General Censure upon other Nightly and Daily Neglects, &c, a copy of which I will endeavour to get. N.B. It was not put into publick Orders. 14th March, 1781.

Thursd 15. Easterly Wind. Cold Day. A Man of the 12th Deserted last Night from Upper Alls Well. This Day all the Real Invilades are order'd to be got Ready to leave this Garrison. N.B. It is said they are to go on board the *Enterprize* this Night.

Fry 16. Easterly Wind. Raining fast in Morning, not much afterwards. I write a long letter this Day to my Sister, as did the Colonel to Mr Fisher; and sent them to the Office; it is supposed they are to go home by the *Enterprize* which is expected to go as this Nt. 3 Men of 56th concerned in a Robery, taken up to Provost.

Saturd 17. Easterly Wind. Soft Morning. The Frigate is not gone. Much Talk of the bad Behaviour of three officers of 12th Regt Relating to a Jew; in Refusing to Pay their Debts; and ill Treatment to the Man, &c. The *Polacre*, Captn McLorg Master, that went up to Minorca in company with the *Hannah* Captn Venture upon the 23rd of Janry, towards the East, came In this Morning, brings a small Quaintity of Casks of Flour, oil and Wine, brings Letters from the Govr of Minorca to our Govr and much Satisfactory News, Relating to our affairs in South America &c. Also brings an Account of the Attack upon Jersey, where we understand the French had made an attempt; and that they were greatly Hurt and drove off.

Sund 18. Easterly Wind. At Day Break it Rained; then held up till near 11. The *Tartar* Cutter, Captn Gibson Master, the same which arrived upon 18th Janry in Mr Turnbulls Employ, and has been a cruize to the East, arrived this Morning, brings some Supplies and fresh confirmation of our having been sending out Troops to the South Seas. The *Enterprize* not gone. I write a letter to my Daughter Helen, as did the Colonel to his Sister, and they all went to the Govrs office.

Mond 19. Easterly Wind; not any Vessels gone. This Day a Small Vessel came In from the East, which proved to be the Tender, belonging to the *Brilliant* Frigate. She was drove from Her anchors in a Gale of Wind, as she lay at Barcelona, and had been a cruize. She has Several Greeks on Board, was drove In by Contrary Winds and much bad Weather, as had the *Tartar* Cutter; who also had a Smartt Engagement with the Enemys Xebeques and Boats, — 9 in all, which He drove off; and Behaved with great Spirit.

Tuesd 20. Easterly Wind. The two Men of the 56th Try'd for a Robery at a Wine House Mans in Irish Town, Colonel Godwin President, Lt Col Cochran, and three Majors and 8 Captains. N.B. It was expected that the three officers of the 12th would have been also Try'd, but the affair with the Jew has been made up. The Whist Meeting, which was to have been at Judge Frazers, was held at Col Craigs. It Rained exceedingly hard all Day and Evening.

1st March, 781.

Wed 21. Easterly Wind. Not any Vessels gone. The Two Men are to be Hang'd. Auctions are now going on every Day, and the Prices of many Articles are greatly Reduced, as for example, Flour, tho' but a small Quaintity ; 200 Wt...22 Drs, Soap 1 R 4 Q per lb., Sugar (soft) 2 Rs pr lb. Beans are now in great plenty, owing to the late Rains. They were at first 4 Rs but now 1 R pr lb. Colliflowers have been Dear, Six and Seven Rials a piece. 3½ Inches of Rain in the last 24 hours,—it is a great happiness to Us.

Thursd 22. Easterly Wind. Fine Morning and Day. A Snow that came In last Sunday from the East, Bound for Liverpool, and who had come In in her way in order to get water, was carried over to Algezira. She had got as far as Caberita point when the Enemy fir'd 5 Shot. However it is conjectured that our own Boats could have brought Her back had they made any Trial. It was a Dead Calm. Mr Aldridch Died this Morning.

Fry 23. Easterly Wind. Raining at Guard Mounting, and continued So all Day. Had a few Friends at dinner, Col Ross, Picton &c, all Well. Some more papers are to be Read to Morrow by the Commanding officers to their Respective Corps, concerning those three young officers of the 12th and their Behaviour to the 2 Jews. It was supposed the affair could not have been so Well made up as it now is, as the offence was of a very Serious Nature, particularly of one of the officers, who had sold his Provisions more than a year agoe to the Jew, for which He Received Money down, and the Man was to have the Provisions, but He has never been able to draw them from the Victing office, owing to our present Circumstances. He therefore wanted his Money back of course, but instead of that was frequently ill used when ever He made any demand, and it was carried so high as to shut him up and Fire, tho' only with Powder, a Pistol at him. This disagreeable Business is finish'd as follows,—and most of it ended thus quietly owing to the Mildness of the Colonel of the Regt and the Govr. The Jew received the full Money, and double Interest for the time, as He made it appear He could have gained many advantages had He been posess'd of the Money, and the three officers gave Ten Guineas each to the Jew. It is hoped this will have a proper Effect upon the Unthinking Young Men who make a custom of ill using any Tradesman who asks for their Money.

Salurd 24. Easterly, a fine soft Morning. The Engineers all mett here at 12 oclock ; and the whole of the Jew Business was explained by order of the Govr and it seems as if it was well taken by every Body not having put it into Garrison Orders. The Colonel up to Willis in afternoon to meet the Govr and did not return till past 11 oclock. N.B. Yesterday We got a hind Qr of Mutton from Genl Boyd : Weight 18 lb, very good Meat.

Sund 25. Easterly Wind, a fine Rain all the forenoon, which will be of the utmost Use to the Gardens. N.B. At this time there is an astonishing plenty of Vegetables, particularly Beans, all owing to the Rain. Col at Mr Holloways this Nt. I was taken very bad with a Complaint in my Head, Jaws, and Teeth, have not been out of my Room since Fryday, and was then very ill, have indeed been in a Daily State of pain and illness for Many Months past, as long as October last but *particularly bad* in Febry and March.

Mond 26. Easterly Wind. Raining a little. Still I am very ill. Col Dined at Genl Boyds, Holloway at Booths. Col at Phipps in Evening. I hear He was in very good Spirits.

Tuesd 27. Easterly Wind. Raining again. My Head very bad. The Whist meeting at Judge Frazers.

Wed 28. Easterly Wind. A Brig coming In from Lisbon was taken over to Algeziras owing to the ill Management of the Master. Mr Ross was on board, and He and the rest of the Crew left the Vessel. He brought In a few Papers, by which We hear of a few alterations. The *Enterprize* and the *Fortune* Sloop sailed in the course of the Nt. The Prize *St. Firmin*, was intended to accompany them, but by some ill Management in geting under sail she Run foul of the Mole Head, so she now remains. Colonel at Captn Eveleghs this Evening. Find myself exceedingly ill indeed.

Thursd 29. Easterly Wind, still raining Hard. Am so very bad with the Complaint in my Mouth as obliged Doctor Baynes to take out a Tooth. Col at Home this Evening. He is now quite Well. A flagg of Truce came with a letter concerning Major Freake of the 39th Regt.

Frv 30. Easterly Wind. Raining soft and easy. Hear that Mr Adair of the 12th had got a Company in the 10th Regt and the Honble Mr Conway of the 39th a Ltcy in the 2nd Battalion of the Royal. Col at Captn Phipps, Stayed rather late. N.B. It is not so Early a Family as our own.

Saturd 31. Easterly Wind ; more soft Rain. Find that the Govr has given Mr Conway leave to go to England, and He is to go In the *Tartar* Cutter which is expected to sail this Evening. I therefore write a letter to my Sister, being willing to take every opportunity. Am still in great pain with my Head and Jaw. Can not go down stairs as yet. My having been so exceedingly indisposed in the Course of the last Ten Days has occasioned my making a few Mistakes, which I mean now to set Right. I have also omitted to mention that the two Unhappy Soldiers of the 56th Regt who were Sentenced to be hang'd both did Suffer upon the Wednesday 28th March.

N.B. I have already mentioned the Vessel from Lisbon being taken over to Algezira, but it was not on Wedy. It was on Thursday forenoon. She had 140 Butts of Wine, some Coals, and other Useful

1st March, 1781.

Articles. By the News papers which Were luckily Saved, We understand that a Convoy is Certainly intended for this place, It seem'd to be ready at the End of Febry. It can not come too Soon, as Numbers of the Inhabitants are in great distress for the Want of Flour. It will become almost impossible to Raise half the Poultry We could wish, owing to the Want of Grain.

*

Sunday April the first. Westerly Wind. A Rainy Night which has brought the Wind to the West. The Cutter did not go last Night. The Guard Mounted at 7 this Morning. It continued Showery all the forenoon *and* Blowing very fresh. Find my Head and Teeth Still very painful. Articles of War Read to every Corps this Day.

Mond 2. Westerly Wind, fine Morning.

Tuesd 3. A Cutter, the *Resolution* arrived from Plymouth, having had a passage of 29 Days. She brings Coals, Rum, Sugar, and other Articles for Government ; and Several letters. We Understand the fleet may be Soon expected. By some letters I hear that the Royals certainly Sailed upon the 28th Novr. Colonel Ross has ask'd Leave of the Govr to go. Barcelo and his Ships seem very busy. Several Xebeques at the Orange Grove. Whist party Col Kellet.

Wed 4. Westerly Wind. The *St Fermin* and all the Vessels gone to the East last Night. Col Ross call'd to ask my Commands for England. He goes in the Cutter which is expected to sail the very first Moment of Fair Wind.† This Evening Lt Burley of the 39th and a party of Soldiers consisting of 30, together with Sailors &c made an attempt In Barges, and Boats to go to Caberitta point in order to Cutt out an arm'd Sloop and some Fire ships as it was said, that have been laying there some few Days. However their Scheme was not altogether Succesfull. It proved a very Stormy Night,—and to conclude this Story, They all came back about three in the Morning, not quite so pleasantly as They went, because at their Return, every one Concerned Seem'd to blame each other. Upon the Second of this Month the following was in orders,—The Soldiers will receive no more Biscuit after this Week, but will receive officers Bread, and the Loaves to be 2 oz heavier.

Thursd 5. Westerly Wind. All the Vessels return In every Night to the Orange Grove. There are two very Large Frigates there. The *Tartar* Cutter not sail'd as yet.

Fry 6. Westerly Wind. All the Same. We do not Fire at all Now,—only by way of Experiments. This Day it was in orders that

---

* Two pages are here left blank, evidently for the other corrections promised above.

† He returned on 13th November, 1781, to command the 72nd Regiment.

all the officers in each Corps are to draw their Provisions all together, 6th April, and that it is to be divided after it is taken from the office. No Body 1781. can tell what Reasons are to be given for this. However it does not give satisfaction to any Body.

Saturd 7. Westerly Wind. About Noon this Day a Vessel appeared from the West. The Gun Boats and the Xebeques went to try and Cutt her off. She got as Near to Europa as she could. The Master behaved Remarkably Well, and as Soon as our Guns could Protect Her all was Well. There were 9 Gun Boats besides other Vessels in pursuit after Her. All the Batterys that Bore that Way Fir'd, and She was got Safe Into the New Mole. She proves to be a Privatter Brig, from Glasgow in 14 Days, the *Eagle*, Captn Crawford, brings a Certainty of the Convoys having sail'd from England upon the 11th of last Month, also very good accounts of a Victory gain'd from the Dutch, Under Sir George Rodney. The arrival of this Vessel has put Us in better Spirits, as We can not doubt of the Convoys being on its Way. N.B. The Corps of Engineers dined at the Govrs this day. I am rather better now.

RATIONS OF PROVISIONS FROM 9TH APRIL TO THE 6TH OF MAY 1781.

Officers a Month. Bread 1 oz pr Day addition ; Beef 4 lb 4 oz ; Pork 4 lb 8 oz ; Butter 10 oz ; Raisons 3 lb ; Pease 2 pints ; Beans 4 Do ; Wheat 4 Do ; Rice 1 Do ; Oil 1 Do.
. 5 lb of Beef, 4 pints of Pease, 12 pints of Oatmeal to be paid for.

Sund 8. Westerly Wind. A very fine Day, quite Warm. All Quiet with us and from the Enemy. A Large Suite of officers were at St Carlos this afternoon.

Mond 9. Easterly Wind. It is expected that the *Tartar* Cutter will go this Evening. Accordingly I write a Duplicate Letter to my Daughter Helen. The Colonel writes to his Sister ; the Jones, &c &c. All those letters went Under Care of Mr Mackellar.

Thursd 12. This Morning at 2 oclock the Col was call'd up to inform Him that a Cutter was come In, from the West, who brings Certain News of the Convoy being just here. She was sent In by Admiral Darby who is Commander in Chief.

(Note : The relieving fleet came in on April 12th and the bombardment began the same day. The Journal only contains the following notes until June 3rd when it is resumed).

Cunningham 39th was wounded on Sunday 22 April ; Died Sunday 6th May,—on Water port Guard. Doctor Chisholm 56 was Wounded, and lost his Leg upon Sunday 15th April.* He was Standing at the

---

* Drinkwater states that on the afternoon of this day the troops in the town began to encamp at the southward and to be distributed in the town casemates.

outside of the casemate Doors in Kings Bast. Lt Boig of the Royal Artillery was Wounded the very first Day of the Firing, Shot in the Shoulder.

Upon Sunday 29th April, 17th Day of Firing, the Enemy had at a Moderate Calculation fired 65,000 Shott and Shells.

Mr Lowe of the 12 Lost his Leg as He was coming down the Steps from Princes Lines, towards the Castle. He was employ'd as an overseer in Kings Work,—Good Man.

Gun Boats came all the time the Fleet was here and then upon the following Days after they went. N.B. They left Gibr (?) 20th April.

23rd first time after the Fleet, between 5 and 6.
30th 13 Boats Kings Bastion.
May 7th in Morning, between 5 and 6, 14 Boats.
Do the 11th, in forenoon 10 oclock.*
Do the 12th in Nt between 12 and 1.   Taken up.†
Do the 20th at 2 in the Morning.   Do.
   24   at 2 in (?) Morning fatal Night. Do.
   26   false alarm.   Taken up.
June 1st at 2 oclock.   Do.
June 3rd at half past one 2 Serjts Killed.   Do.

They are always attended by Mortar Boats. When they come at Nt they always fire a Shell first, about 10 Minutes, and then begin with Shott and Shells. Their signal for Retreating at Night is throwing up Rockets.

Their Balls 26 lbs...Shells 13 Inch. They are about 40 Ft each Boat and carry 18 Rounds each,—Mortar Boats 12 Rounds. Upon the 31st in the Morning They fired 49 Shells, 190 Ball, and a Barr Shott of 35 lb Wt went Into a Large Tent belonging to the Qr Master Genl quite through the Tent; but did not do any hurt,—a very Remarkable Shott came Into our Garden about 10 Yards from the Bow Window. It fell upon a small Walling of stone, about 8 Inches high which was a sort of Bordering. The Shott broke into a Number of pieces, Drove a piece of the Stone Wall up into the Room, breaking the Glass of Bow Window. N.B. I have taken home a Large piece of this Shott, it being Esteem'd a Curiosity in its kind. N.B. The Garrison fir'd Grape shott, as well as shell and it was supposed must have greatly hurt them—2 Hours.

* On this date Drinkwater says " Scarcely a house north of the Grand Parade was tenantable."

† Probably these words refer to Mrs. Green—being an invalid—having to be taken up and carried to the Bomb-proof. See entry below under date June 3.

After the first fortnights Fire, the Enemy began to Slacken Fire. It was often 1,700 Rounds a Day,—particularly the beginning of May.

Upon or about the latter end of May they came down to 400 Rounds the Day,—particularly that was the Number upon Fryday 1st June.

A Jew Woman, a Man, and Young Lad, were kill'd on the Nt of the 23rd May by a Shell from Gun Boats, as were also three other men, and Many Wounded. We did not fire at all, as the Govr had Express'd Disapprobation at our firing on some other occasions. They Seem'd to be about half a Mile distant at one time upon the 31st May ; but after that, somewhat nearer before they were drove off. The Large Howitzer upon Buena Vista distress't them a good deal this Night. *Enterprize* went out on Sunday Night 27th May. The *Flora* and *Crescent*, Frigates from Minorca went through on Monday Morning 28th. N.B. The Splinters of a Shell struck the Tin funnel of the Stove in Bomb Proof upon the Nt of 31st.

N.B. Omitted to mention that upon Monday 7th May the Gun Boats fired 345 Rounds of Ball and Shells. N.B. To be attentive in puting down these Memᵃ and to place them in proper dates in order to avoid Confusion. A Ragusian came In on Thursday 31st May and was brought to by the Garrison.

June 3rd. Easterly Wind. Upon Saturday Night, or Sunday Morning at half past one the Gun Boats came, and began in a most Violent Manner. It was with much difficulty I was taken into the Bomb Proof. The Enemy fired more than ever. They came very close. *We* fir'd from the Garrison and a little from Shiping. We had 2 Serjants kill'd and Several others Wounded. It is hardly possible for pen, or even Words, to describe the distress and hurry this business puts us into.

This Day Sunday 3rd June, a very Large Fleet going through. We have heard of this by other means, but it appears very formidable. The Grand Hospital much affected last Night. Upon June 1st more than 200 men Wounded and 60 Dead of their Wounds, besides a Number of Inhabitants who have been Kill'd.

Mond 4. Royal Standard up at Grand Battery. By Noon the Enemy had sent three Balls through it. At one oclock We Fired every piece of Ordnance that Bore upon the advanc'd Work, being 65. No very material hurt was done to the Enemy's Works. The Day being Damp and an Easterly Wind it is supposed had some effect upon the Powder. About 2 there came round from the East a Line of Battle Spainish Man of War, 4 Xebeques and 2 Bomb Ketches, and went to Algezira. Many persons believed that the Line of

4th June,
1781.

Battle Ship would have given a Broad Side to the *Brilliant* Frigate as
she came very close, but all was quiet. N.B. The Gun Boats have
been Commanded by Don Juan Moreno, of the Rank of Major Genl.
This We heard by means of some Spainish Gazettes which came down
from Minorca. N.B. Barcelo has been gone ever since the Firing.

Tuesd 5. Easterly Wind. All quiet from the Gun Boats, but a
good deal of Firing keep up from the Enemy. It is now to be fear'd
that the two India Men will be detained some time longer; as those
ships laying over at Algezira is much against their going out. I am
very indifferent still, and with much difficulty can get down stairs.

When the family were going to Bed, between 11 and 12 an Alarm
was given from the Guard Boats, and instantly the whole Camps were
up, and the Artillery went to the Batterys &c. I went down to the
Bomb proof instead of going to Bed; had the Child taken up, a Fire
made in Bomb Proof, and every thing made as Comfortable as it
could be, every Moment expecting the Gun Boats. We all knew that
one of the Line of Battle Ships had gone to nearer the Orange Grove
in the Day, and it was thought she was Under sail in the Evening
which led us to suppose she was to assist the Boats, but all was quiet
from them.

Wed 6. Westerly Wind. A good deal of Firing as Usual. Could
not make myself Easy in the Evening, therefore went again to Bomb
Proof,—all quiet.

Thursd 7. Westerly. Cold Blowing Day. Am not quite so Lame
as I have been ; find myself growing very Tired and indisposed in the
Evening. Therefore went to Bed before 10. A little before 11 an
alarm was given of Vessels being coming very near our Batterys. It
was Supposed it was either Fire Ships, or Bomb Ketches. In consequence all the Troops got up and went to those places appointed for
Safety, except those on Duty. I was obliged to be taken out of Bed,
and away again to Bomb Proof. This Disagreed with me more than
I can express. Our Suspense Continued till past 12, and then it was
clearly found to be 3 or 4 Xebeques that was going out after 2 Vessels
which sail'd for Minorca.

Fry 8. Westerly Wind. All has remained quiet. I find myself
exceedingly ill, the whole Day, indeed Uncommonly So,—obliged to
go to Bed after dinner, and Dreadfully alarm'd lest the Gun Boats
should come this Night ; as I am realy too bad to bear the Moving.
However they Luckily did not ; and We all got a good Nights Sleep.

Saturd 9. Westerly Wind ; Cold and Blowing hard. About 11 a
very Loud Explosion was heard, and a very heavy discharge of shells,
with the Utmost Rapidity from the Enemy's Camp. It was Instantly
Seen to proceed from an accident amongst themselves. Their
principal Laboratory Tent, under the Queen of Spains Chair, near the
Catalan Camp, Blew up,—also a Building near to it. The fire was
Violent ; and extended to a Large Heap of Live shells, which Blew

up in a most furious Manner. Nothing could equal the Confusion the 9th June, Enemy were In. This Tent is about four Thousand, five Hundred 1781. Yards from Landport. They beat to Arms. Their whole Line turn'd out under arms. It enabled our officers to form some Idea of the Number of Troops ; which by observing the Number of Battalions seems by all accounts to amount to 10,000 men. Their Commander; in Chief was Seen Riding with the Utmost Speed, attended by all his Suite in equal haste, towards where the accident happened. I plainly saw the poor Men Runing from the Flames. It continued Burning an hour and half and the bursting of the Shells more than half an hour. This accident must have done them most Essential hurt ; and of course lower'd the Ammunition greatly. The Line of Battle Ship which Lay near the Orange Grove sent all Her People on shore to assist, and 6 Gun Boats went from Algezira to the Orange Grove.

Soon after the accident the Enemy Fir'd a Shott from a 14 Gun Battery up to Williss. It came through the Embrasure ; Kill'd one Artillery Man, blowing him to pieces. He fell upon an other who was Mortaly Wounded. 2 other Artillery Men were also Wounded by the Same Ball, but it is hoped they will Recover.

A LIST OF THE KILLED AND WOUNDED, FROM APRIL 12TH TO THE 4TH JUNE.

Killed. 6 Serjants, 1 Corporal, 1 Drum, 37 Private ; Total, 45.
Died of their Wounds. 1 officer, Lt Cunningham of the 39th Regt, 1 Serjant, 16 private ; Total, 18.
Wounded. 8 officers, 1 Surgeon, 1 Do Mate, 16 Serjants, 15 Corporals, 5 Drums, 201 Private ; Total, 247.
Officers Names. Lt Lowe of 12th Lost His Leg, Surgeon of 56th Lost His Leg.

A Remarkable Event happened upon the 22nd of May ; which I omitted to set down in its proper place ; must therefore now Mention it.

At 2 oclock in the Morning, a Shell thrown from the Enemy, fell upon a Gun on the Church Battery, Line Wall, burst as it fell ; a Splinter of which went to the South Bastion 360 Yds from Church Battery, and Cutt the Leaden Apron that Cover'd the Vent ; and Fir'd the Morning and Evening Gun.

The Evening after the above a shell fell upon the Grand Battery, the bursting of which Fir'd one of the Guns, which Gun was Loaded with Grape shott and Laid for the Gardens. N.B. The Enemy are every Night in the Gardens and it is remarkable enough that one of their own Shells should be the Means of Sending those Grape shott amongst them ; by way of Saving us the Trouble. Lt Cuppage of Royal Artillery was on the Flagg Staff Guard at the time.

10th June,
1781.

Sund 10. Westerly Wind. This Morning about 7 the Line of Battle Ship came from the Orange Grove. The wind brought Her near to our Guns, and the Garrison fir'd at Her from Kings Bastion. Several shot struck Her. She sheer'd off and went to Algezira. The Enemy Fir'd a Good deal this Day. Went as Usual to Bomb proof.

Mond 11. Westerly wind. This Morning about 7 a Flagg of Truce came from the Enemy, informing us of our having made a mistake Yesterday ; as it was a N—* Man of War that We Fir'd at. This Evening Mr Ward saild In an Arm'd Vessel call'd the *General Murray,* for Minorca. I wrote to my Son and my Sister.

Tuesd 12. Westerly wind. This Morning at half past one the Gun and Mortar Boats came as Usual. There seem'd to be a good Number. They were Fir'd at from every part that Bore upon them. The shiping also gave them a Warm Reception. Several of their shells burst in the air ; one over our House ; and the Fuzee Remains upon the Top of it. They Staid a little better than an Hour. An Unlucky accident happened in a Tent belonging to a soldier of the 56th. His wife, a very Good Young Woman, and a Young child of three months were Blown out of the Tent by a Shell. They were thrown into a Deep Gully, and Child Torn to pieces and the Woman much Burnt and otherwise Wounded. A Man this Day of the Working party kill'd at Willisses,—and in the last three Days 4 or 5 have been Killed.

Wed 13. Westerly Wind ; all quiet from Gun Boats.

(The diary ends here abruptly, Mrs. Green's failing health probably rendering her no longer equal to writing after June 13th. She left the Rock and returned to England on the 22nd July, 1781, and died there on the 21st of June in the following year).

* This is left blank in the diary but Drinkwater states the ship was a Neapolitan.

www.ingramcontent.com/pod-product-compliance
Lightning Source LLC
Chambersburg PA
CBHW020611160726
47991CB00002BA/727